QUEST

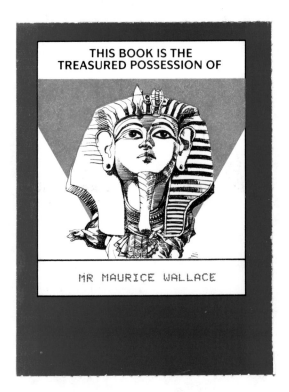

THIS BOOK IS THE TREASURED POSSESSION OF

MR MAURICE WALLACE

QUEST

STEPHEN L. CARMAN
with BOB OWEN

Tyndale House
Publishers, Inc.
Wheaton, Illinois

Second printing, December 1986

Library of Congress Catalog Card Number 86-50566
ISBN 0-8423-5112-4
Printed in the United States of America

I dedicate this book to my loving wife, Joan,
and my three super children, Scott, Sheri, and Chris,
who make the story of my life worth telling.

CONTENTS

PREFACE

As I write this preface, divers are probing the depths of the ocean near Cape Canaveral for remnants of the Space Shuttle *Challenger,* which exploded shortly after launch on January 28, 1986. The loss of the seven crew members in this disaster stunned me as well as the whole nation. Indeed, the whole world. My heart reaches out to the team of engineers and scientists most closely involved in this mission, as it brings back memories of our first space project disaster, which I describe in the opening chapters of this book.

I share in part your horror, anguish, and sense of defeat. Yet I am certain of one thing: the cause for this tragedy will be found and corrected so that subsequent missions will be safer for those who follow.

God has allowed man to probe into space, to realize its vastness and the uniqueness of our planet Earth among the universe. As we continue learning more and more about the universe, it becomes clearer that it must have had an intelligent creator. I finally came to know this creator from his space, drawn to his light in his perfect time.

Actually, this whole book is a "preface." When I first met with the Tyndale House editors to discuss the possibility of writing a book I had outlines on the subject of the Bible and science. The editors reviewed the material and decided there were enough ideas for several books. I was elated!

But they also were intrigued with my testimony, and decided I should first document the amazing story of how an atheistic scientist and his Jewish wife came to accept Christ as their Lord and Savior. "We need a 'where you're coming from' book," they told me, "to introduce you and your background."

So, with the help of Bob Owen who patiently converted many hours of recorded interviews into the chapters that follow, we now share our story. And there is an excitement in my heart as I read through these pages and recall more clearly than ever how God has had his hand on my life, even when I didn't believe he existed.

My hope is that you will enjoy this story, but more importantly that you will come to realize that there is a spiritual part of you that yearns to know the same God I have come to know. My career in the nation's major space programs always presents me with challenges, and I am continually aware of my reliance on my faith in God, and always ready to share my testimony of his love.

Now, with this book, I can share it with many whom I will never meet.

Steve Carman
Proverbs 3:5, 6

1

TRAGEDY
AT THE CAPE

On that fateful day—January 27, 1967—my office
phone rang as I prepared to leave for home. When I
picked it up, a hoarse, hardly recognizable voice asked,
"Steve, have you heard about the fire?"

"What fire?"

"Here . . . at the Cape."

I recognized the voice of Gary Frye, the lead electrical engineer who had traveled to Kennedy Space Center with Apollo 1. He and I and our wives had become
friends during my last stay at the Cape. Gary was obviously distraught.

I felt my stomach knot. "No . . . what happened?"

"Pad 34 . . . prelaunch testing. Fire broke out in the
crew compartment of the command module. Apollo 1."

"In the crew compartment?" Instantly my mind envi-
sioned the interior of the tiny Apollo capsule, which I
knew better than my own home. Picturing the interior
from the opened hatch I panned across the hundreds of

switches on the control panel to the crew couches. And in my mind I saw the faces of the astronauts I had trained—Gus Grissom on the left, Ed White in the middle, Roger Chaffee on the right.

"Was anybody hurt?"

"Steve, they're dead. All three astronauts—Grissom, Chaffee, and White—burned to death. Or asphyxiated when the high-pressure oxygen in the closed capsule caught fire. They didn't even have time to open the hatch."

I slumped back in my chair. "Oh, my God . . ." The paradox of this use of God's name didn't strike me at the moment, because in my heart I didn't believe there was a God. Yet as I desperately sought to comprehend the magnitude of this tragedy, the phrase somehow seemed appropriate.

Gary went on talking, but I caught only snatches of what he was saying. "Prelaunch test . . . simulating translunar environment . . . test not considered hazardous since rocket fuels had not been loaded . . . so no emergency personnel standing by . . . that flash of fire in the window . . . the men's screams, 'Get us out of here!' . . ."

His flow of words ceased abruptly. There was a catch in his breath as he resumed. "Steve, it's a real mess in there. They won't let anybody get in . . . the mission's scrubbed . . . full investigation to follow . . ."

Mercifully, he finally stopped talking. "Steve. Steve? Are you still there?"

"Yeah," I said weakly, feeling stunned, not knowing what to say. "I'm here."

Then I asked the obvious question. "What caused the fire?"

He didn't answer immediately, and when he did, he

spoke slowly, cautiously. "Well . . . nobody knows for sure . . . not absolutely for sure. But the pad leader thinks it *might have been* a spark . . . from some faulty wiring, or the test batteries."

After he assured me there was nothing I could do at the Cape, I thanked him for calling and we hung up.

All at once it hit me. *All three of the astronauts are dead!* Gus Grissom . . . Ed White . . . Roger Chaffee. The first Apollo crew . . . all of them dead.

I stared at their pictures on my office wall. There they were, just as I knew them. Or as I *had known* them. I choked at the past tense.

I thought of the men's wives. Surely they would already have been informed of their loss. How unbelieving, how horrified they must be. I imagined their anger too, and their frustration. For, even more so than their men, they had trusted in our ability to keep them safe. And we had failed them all. Failed them even before the men left the earth. Not en route to the moon in the alien and hostile environment of space, but here on earth. *On the launchpad!*

Never before had such a catastrophe stricken America's manned space flights. I thought of Mercury and Gemini. Hadn't the safety measures that surrounded them established adequate safety procedures for today's prelaunch tests? Or had our previous successes blunted our awareness to both the magnitude and the hazards of this all-consuming quest to put men on the moon?

Suddenly I felt ashamed. Ashamed as though *I* was personally responsible for this tragedy. And, at least to a degree, perhaps I was. After all, I had helped to train the crew and had supervised the North American Rockwell personnel of the test team. Had I overlooked some vital detail, some crucial step in the complex pre-launch procedures?

In that awful moment I realized that the perfection I had always prided myself for—that I had *insisted on* from my team of engineers—would now be overshadowed with a dark cloud. As, indeed, would the entire space program.

What would be the public's reaction to this tragedy? Would public outcry force Congress and the president to halt America's participation in the space race?

All at once I felt the compulsion to go home, to be with my wife, to talk to her. When I arrived, Joanie listened intently to the news of the tragedy and did her best to comfort me and calm my fears. Later that evening, we watched news reports about the fire on television. The cameras showed the Apollo still on the launchpad, but showed no pictures of the interior.

The news commentator repeated the taped final words of the trapped men. It was awful beyond description.

We went to bed, but sleep wouldn't come. Joanie and I talked late into the night. I told her about my conversation with the librarian and her optimism about Apollo's future. "I know we've lost men in similar research before," I said, "and we've had close calls . . . such as that fuel-cell failure on Gemini V, and the thruster failure on Gemini VIII. But in each case we got the crews back safely . . . and so far we've never lost a man in the space program. . . ." I stared at the blackness of our bedroom. "Until now."

Lying beside me Joanie was getting drowsy, but I still felt a nearly desperate urge to talk, almost to myself. "And putting a man on the moon demands that *everything's* got to work right. The first time." I groaned in anguish.

Joanie stirred and awakened a little. "What's wrong, Steve?"

"I'm almost sure there'll be serious setbacks from this fire."

"Like what?"

"I don't know. Maybe it'll mean a year's delay to re-design and rebuild. Or even cancellation of the whole program!"

The thought of starting over again was almost as distasteful to me as cancellation. I'd put in so much time on the project. But on the other hand, there were several changes we'd like to make. Maybe, just maybe, if we started again from scratch, we could somehow redeem the project, and the lives of these three men would not have been in vain. And the tragedy would result in safer spacecraft for future astronauts. . . .

At the moment even that possibility brought little comfort. I sighed into the darkness. "There's nothing that can make it right. Not for those men, not for their families. Those men are dead, and that's that."

My mind was still whirling. I'd already gone over every single minute detail of the program a dozen times that day. The whole approach to spacecraft testing—especially with the crew—was already so controlled, right down to the finest detail, that I just didn't know how to improve it.

"Joanie," I said bitterly, "it boils down to this: some-body made a mistake . . . and maybe it was me."

She was suddenly completely awake. "But you weren't even there! How could you be blamed?"

"Maybe my crew training wasn't good enough.

Maybe those procedures that I wrote left something out. And maybe I'm not cut out for this kind of work."

Then I expressed the thought that had persisted all day. "And even if Apollo doesn't end here, I'm not sure that I want to go on . . . I'm just not sure."

"Go to sleep, Steve," Joanie said. "You're very tired. Maybe things will look different tomorrow."

It was unusual for me to be so pessimistic, but it seemed impossible for me to shake the great sense of loss I felt. For the past couple of years my work had been a haven from which I could escape the pain of the death of my parents. Now . . .

2

A
RAILROAD
MAN

Donald LaVerne Carman, my father, an only child, was a very creative and versatile man. Mother, Nevada Margaret DeVaney, was a beautiful, petite blond, the youngest of eight children. Born in Utah, she and her family shortly thereafter moved to the tiny town of Wells, Nevada, where she lived until she met my father.

The two met when my father was passing through Wells on a hunting trip. The beauty of this young lady caught his eye. After a brief courtship, against the wishes of their parents, they were married in Reno. Dad quit high school and went to work to support himself and his bride. They were just seventeen, and the year was 1940.

Some years later, while working for the railroad, a near tragedy provided Dad with an unexpected opportunity for advancement. While working in the railroad roundhouse one day, he walked past one of the old reciprocating steam engines just as a relief valve shot forth a heavy blast of live steam. The superheated steam instantly enveloped both legs, fusing his coveralls to his flesh and transforming his legs into solid blisters.

It was a miracle Dad didn't lose his legs. In the hospital, his clothes had to be cut off. When he was released from the hospital, his legs were in such bad condition that Dad could no longer load boxcars or work as a mechanic. So he was offered an office job as a timekeeper.

That particular timekeeper's job consisted simply of collecting and organizing time cards, then tallying the hours and computing the men's wages. Always well-organized, Dad soon realized that he was spending much of his time transferring information onto numerous, often confusing forms, records, and cards. So he periodically brought them all home with him and spread them out on our dining room table.

I watched him shift them around like chessmen, lean back and look at them, then move them again, making notes on several as he did so. Then one by one, as he sketched new, simpler forms, Dad began removing the old forms and cards from the table. Before long he had eliminated a dozen or so of the older forms and consolidated them into one of his own design.

When Dad instituted the new form in his record keeping, the change was soon noticed by top management. And he was invited to the larger office as an accountant for the entire Freight Division of Western Pacific Railroad. I was about nine years old at the time. We moved to Sacramento to live in half of a duplex a short distance from the old state fairgrounds, where we lived for five or six years while Dad continued to work his particular brand of magic on everything he touched. Because of Dad's ability to simplify and consolidate procedures and forms, the railroad created a new position for him, gave him the title of "Forms Analyst," and moved him to the head office in San Francisco.

Computers were in their infancy at the time, and until then had been used primarily for accounting purposes. Western Pacific sent Dad to an IBM-operated computer school to learn everything about them he could. It was a wise move. Dad not only helped implement use of computers in the accounting department, but also instituted the first computer tracking system in the entire railroad industry.

With his system, Dad was soon able to track and locate any shipment on the railroad and report to any customer the exact whereabouts of his product, along with precise information about when he could expect his shipment of chickens, corn, automobiles, or whatever else he may have shipped.

Dad's reward for his revolutionary computer implementation was advancement to the position of Purchasing Agent in Western Pacific's headquarters office.

With models such as my parents, it's no wonder I was an achiever in school. In fact, I always did so well in my classes that when I was in the sixth or seventh grade my teacher recommended that I take an IQ test. Apparently I scored very well, because the teacher made an appointment with my parents one evening and had a long discussion with them.

After she had talked for what seemed ages to me, my father responded, "Well, I thank you for coming. That's a very good report on my son. But what are you going to do with it?"

The teacher cleared her throat. "Mr. Carman, it's evident to us that Steve has special ability, that he's gifted. And we think Steve should be sent to a private school, one for children who possess unusual potential. The classes will be smaller, and he'll be able to obtain the accelerated learning that he should be getting."

I saw my father shaking his head. "No."

She looked startled. "No? You mean . . . ?"

"That's right. I know Steve's a bright boy. But if he was to get into a school with all other bright kids, he might miss what life is all about. Steve's going to rub elbows with average kids all his life. So why should he spend several years in a school where he'll be cloistered away from average kids now? I thank you for your kind words and for your interest in Steve, but I want him in public school right where he is."

I appreciated Dad's stand, but it still left me in a position where I always got A's without having to struggle for them.

It was while I was in junior high school in Sacramento that I made a tentative decision to become an engineer. It was also during that time I came to the conclusion that what I most liked to do was to take things apart, study how they were made, sometimes design improvements, and put them back together again. Since I loved anything that had to do with tools, mechanisms, and electronics, it was no wonder that aptitude tests indicated engineering would be a possible career for me.

I spent most of my allowance at war surplus stores, where I bought anything that looked like it could be disassembled. And our garage soon took on the appearance of the surplus stores from which most of the stuff came.

I think my engineering career decision was greatly influenced by an engineer neighbor who lived in the

other half of the duplex we lived in. We talked often
and he told me about his work, which sounded interesting, like something I might enjoy.

One day he gave me an old textbook titled *Man's
Physical Universe*. Published in the forties, the book
covered about every science subject you could think
of—from radios to the solar system, along with everything else in between.

But it wasn't until we moved to San Francisco in
1957 that I really studied that book. There, with the
book in hand, I would often walk across the street to
the park and read it from cover to cover. Then I would
start at the beginning again and read it through several
times, utterly fascinated with each subject.

"Where have you been all day?" my father asked me
once after I'd been soaking in that book all day.

"In the park."

"In the park? All day? What were you doing in the
park?"

"Reading."

"Reading! You're always reading. Why don't you
spend time with girls? Go to a dance or a movie or
something?"

I shrugged. "Because I'd rather read." Actually I was
a lousy dancer, and I looked upon most of the activities
of my peers as a waste of time. Though I was as attracted to girls as any teenager, I was too shy to begin a
relationship. Besides, I cherished the time I spent learning the many, many facts about the world around us.

My engineer neighbor encouraged my attitude of
continual learning, and I remember hearing him say,
"You never know when it's going to come in handy."

I loved my tools and electronic "junk." And it was
my joy to gather a bunch of broken-down radios and

repair them. My parents didn't seem to mind, as long as I didn't keep my stuff strewn all over the house. Mostly I worked in my room, but occasionally my "things" would be strung from room to room.

Nobody taught me anything about electricity or radio repair. But I learned—by getting shocked a few times—that there are some things you don't do with a "hot wire." I didn't have a workbench as such, but I did have a large bin where I kept all my stuff. Whenever I had any nuts and bolts, screws or nails, condensers or tuners, I just dropped them into my bin. And whenever I needed anything for one of my projects, I was usually successful in digging around until I found it.

I built my own radio antenna by putting up three high poles in our backyard and stringing copper wire from one to the other. Then at night I'd "D-X," or try to see how many different and distant cities I could bring in on my hopped-up, amplified receiver. After a few months the map over my bed was filled with thumbtacks that marked the outer limits of my receiving.

One night I was twiddling with the dial when I picked up a very faint station. Thinking it just *might* be a more distant station than any I had picked up before, I checked its frequency in the radio station handbook. When I found no local station at that frequency, I was certain that this was a new and distant station. I had read enough about radio waves to know that when clouds and weather were just right for signals to bounce off the ionosphere, signals could travel for fantastic distances.

I held my breath and listened for the station call letters. Characteristic of these skip conditions, the signal faded in and out, occasionally fading altogether. I heard music, then the announcer's voice. I strained my ears. Suddenly I caught the call letters and the magical words, ". . . coming to you from Niagara Falls. . . ."

My whoop must have wakened my parents, because at breakfast the next morning my father spoke from behind his morning *San Francisco Examiner* and asked, "What was all the commotion about last night . . . after you were supposed to be asleep?"

"I tuned in Niagara Falls last night," I explained.

"That's good," he said, and went right on reading the paper.

I was hurt. "Good? Dad, that's a record for me. Niagara Falls is nearly three *thousand* miles away."

He was slightly more impressed and put down his paper to peer at me over his glasses. "Then that's *very good*, Steve! Congratulations!" With those words, I was satisfied with my accomplishment. It was always extremely important to me that my parents, especially my father, approved of my doings.

In many homes Sunday was the day to go to church. But not in our home. Sunday was a day for "catching up" on things you couldn't get done the other six days of the week. During baseball season Dad coached a Little League team, and my brother and I would practice baseball on Sunday.

As a girl, my mother had gone to a small Episcopal church in the Nevada community where she was raised. She was teaching Sunday school there when she and my father met. She always felt that we should go to church. But Dad had been raised by a Catholic stepmother who was adamant about his weekly attendance at mass. Church to him had become associated with a lot of negative things; so he rebelled against it. He said

23

he didn't get anything from it and didn't believe in it. So Dad decided that when he had a family, they would not attend church.

Mother honored Dad's decision and refrained from taking us to church—except for one time. When we lived in Sacramento, a new church was built close to us, and Mother thought it would be nice if we went to Sunday school to check it out.

She got me bathed, and I dressed in my best clothes. She drove me to the church and let me out in front. I was really scared. This was a totally new experience, and I didn't know what to expect. So it was with great trepidation that I made my way up the steps to the entryway. Just before I entered the foyer, I turned and looked back. Mother was still parked at the curb.

When I got inside, I didn't know what to do. I just stood there, poised like a bird getting ready for flight, when an usher approached me. In my already tremulous state, the man looked like a huge, formidable guard, and his voice sounded gruff and challenging.

"What do you want, sonny?" he asked.

That was all I needed. I turned and fled. My mother was just driving away. "Wait! Wait!" I shouted, running down the sidewalk after her. Fortunately she heard me and stopped. I was trembling when I got in the car.

"What's the matter?" she asked.

"That man scared me."

That traumatic incident both initiated and concluded our "family church attendance." And until long after I was married, those few moments in that church foyer represented the sum total of my church experience. Nothing much was ever said about my adventure into the church world, and my Sundays settled back into a comfortable routine: I practiced baseball with my brother.

To my knowledge, there was never any real conflict between my parents on the subject of religion, because, aside from this isolated incident, neither the Bible nor church were ever mentioned in our home. Consequently, I never had the slightest awareness that either one could possibly present any relevance to life in general or to my own life in particular.

As a result, I grew up as totally ignorant of God and the Bible as any untouched, undiscovered aborigine in the interior of Australia, or any other continent. It wasn't that I didn't believe in God so much as the fact that I didn't know there was anything to believe in. I was a total, unmitigated atheist. I just didn't know anything else, or any other way to live or to believe.

Years later when I was filling out my application for the University of California at Berkeley, I came to the blank that asked me to state my religious preference. I didn't know what to say. So I showed it to my father.

"Just write Protestant," he said. "That's general enough. That tells them that you're not a Jew."

Though we never talked much about religion in our home, we all knew my father's position on the subject: he looked down on anything to do with religion or religious life. "Religion is for people who need a crutch," he said. "And I've never needed a crutch, so I've never turned to religion."

When people asked me about religion, I would tell them, "You can believe what you want to believe, but there really isn't a God. God is just a creation of man."

"Don't you mean, *God* created man?"

I shook my head. "No, it was man who created God. He's just a god of the mysterious, the things man can't explain scientifically. When man couldn't understand the world he lived in, he simply created God as the ultimate explanation. Like the Greeks with their gods of fire and love and war. When science explained fire to be merely an oxidation process, the need for God was dissolved. Science will eventually provide the explanation for all mysteries. Then there won't be any need for God."

I wasn't antagonistic toward religious people. I just thought they were strange, or that they were mindlessly following tradition for tradition's sake. "One day science will explain all those 'unknowables' around us," I said, "and when that happens, there won't be any need for a residual God."

These responses came mainly from my home environment, and when I went to Berkeley these ideas were amplified and expanded as evolutionary thought pervaded all the technical subjects I studied.

Personally I thought, *If I ever have need of a religion, there are plenty from which to choose.* At that time—if ever such a time would come—I thought I could study them all and select the best one for me.

Despite the absence of religious training, our home was a good place. It was full of warmth and love. My mother's care and teaching of my brother and me were strongly biblically based and moral in every respect. Both she and Dad instilled into us the necessity of doing our best in everything we did.

We were taught the importance of proper manners and respect for others. If a person came to our home, his station in life made no difference. Rich or poor, influential or otherwise, he was to be treated with dignity.

Since there were no girls in the family, my mother

taught my brother and me how to cook and clean. Both of us learned how to make bread and cakes, how to plan and prepare meals, and how to wash and iron and do all the chores around the house. Between my mother and us two boys, our home was always immaculate.

I was very proud of my parents, my father in particular. As a result of their achievements, and my pride in them, I directed my whole life to please them.

3

SOPHOMORE EXPERIENCE

It happened during my sophomore year, when my roommate began dating a girl named Joan. "You should meet her," John raved. "She's a lot of fun."

At the moment I wasn't interested in a girl. But the UCLA/Cal football game was coming up, and John asked a favor. "Steve, will you please help me out and double-date with Joan and me and her friend from Los Angeles?"

I reluctantly agreed and a few days later met Joan and her friend Sarah.

Although I was to escort Sarah, I was attracted to Joan, and spent more time getting acquainted with her than I did with Sarah. When it started to rain, Joan and I shared an umbrella, leaving Sarah with John.

I learned that Joan was Jewish. She was from the Los Angeles area and was majoring in education. John's description was right: Joan *was* fun to be with. But he hadn't told me the half of it. Not only was Joan fun; she was beautiful. With a bright smile and a quick sense of humor, she was a delight to be around. Furthermore, she also seemed to be interested in me.

But I was too busy to be seriously interested. However, in subtle ways Joan managed to cultivate our relationship. And I was enjoying it. One day when she and I met as I was on my way to the library, Joan asked me to return her overdue books.

"Sure, I'll drop them off," I told her. She handed me the money, and I put it in my pocket. When I returned the books and paid the fine, I discovered that Joan had given me much too much money. I called her and told her that I had some change for her.

She said, "Just keep it until I see you again."

I said, "Okay . . . meet me for coffee." And she agreed. Later I learned that she had planned the whole episode just so we could be together. What a disappointing evening it must have been for her. All I did was talk about *my* interests and *my* plans, and scarcely talked about her. But apparently what Joan saw she liked, and she stopped dating John. (I didn't learn this until much later.)

Despite my seeming lack of interest, we managed to meet a number of times before the school year ended. But each time we were together it was the same thing: all I talked about was *me* and *mine,* and little about her and hers. During the summer we went our separate ways, she back to Los Angeles and me back to San Francisco. But I couldn't forget her. And as the school year drew near, I became more and more eager to return to Berkeley to see her. It was a busy time for me, because I had rented an off-campus room for my junior year and was busily preparing to move from my parents' home in San Francisco.

My father's car, which I had borrowed for the move,

was jammed with my books and clothes, but I still had room for our neighbor's daughter, a first-year student at Berkeley.

Joan had also been eagerly awaiting her return to school. But when I drove past the dorms, she happened to see me and my pretty passenger. Her natural female assumption was that I had gotten involved with the young lady and that we had gotten married during the summer. All her hopes and plans for a future with me were dashed to the ground.

As soon as she could, she telephoned John. After they had chatted for a few minutes, she asked, "Did Steve get married this summer?"

John chuckled. "Steve? No way. We've been in touch this summer. He's not even serious about anybody."

When I learned from John that Joan was asking about me, I was excited. I called her and asked her for a date. She consented, and from the beginning of the year we were together on an almost daily basis. We found ourselves mutually compatible, and our relationship flourished.

On several occasions I took Joan to my parents' home for a visit. They loved her, but advised against marriage until after graduation. Joan was eager for me to meet her family in Los Angeles and arranged for me to go home with her during Easter vacation in 1964.

". . . and you can take part in Passover seder."

"That'll be great!" I said. "I'm eager to meet your family."

She agreed, but I could tell she was nervous about the meeting. I asked her why.

"Well, every time I've met a man I liked, he's been a goy. And my folks have never approved of my dating a goy."

31

"A goy?" I asked. "What's a goy?" I thought I could assure her that there were certainly no goys in my family.

She laughed. "A goy is a Gentile. Someone who's not a Jew."

"Oh," I said, somewhat deflated. "Well, the shoe fits. I guess I am a goy." Then it was my turn to be nervous. "Do you think your parents will forbid you to see me again?"

Joan shook her head. "No . . . my mother already likes you."

"But we haven't even met."

"But I've talked to her about you many times. She likes you because I like you. She just wants to meet you."

"And your father?"

Joan shook her head again. "No problem there. The one I'm nervous about is my grandmother."

I was incredulous. "Your grandmother?"

"Yes. If she says I can't see you . . . well, that's it."

"You mean your *grandmother* has that much say in the way you run your life?" All of this sounded like something out of an ancient European society, not the twentieth century.

"Yes," Joan said, "she's a typical Jewish grandmother . . . she's very protective of her granddaughter. And I'm sure the rest of the family will accept whatever Grandmother says."

Now it was my time to get nervous. And I soon shared Joan's concern about the upcoming trip. Would Joan's grandmother reject me as she had the other goys Joan had known?

Joan and I rode from Berkeley to her parents' apartment near UCLA with a friend, arriving in Westwood in the late afternoon. As soon as we drove up and began unloading, Joan's mother saw us and dashed out to meet us.

"Steve, this is Bess, my mom," Joan said as her mother gave us both a squeeze and a kiss. "And, Mom, this is Steve."

"Joan has told me all about you. I've been waiting to meet you." She took me by the hand. "Come in . . . come in!" Inside, I met Joan's stepfather, a quiet man who reminded me of my father. They all put me at ease, and within minutes I felt like this was a reunion of long-lost friends.

During a pause, Joan asked, "How is Grandmother?"

"She's fine. I told her you were coming. And she wants us to come to her place tomorrow. Okay?"

"Sure . . . fine," Joan said. Her smile and the touch of her hand assured me, *It'll be all right.*

As we entered Joan's grandmother's home the next day, my nostrils were assailed by the aroma of cooking food. When Joan introduced me to the cheerful, sprightly woman, I said, "Something smells good. What is it?"

Her face brightened. "Come see," she said, separating me from Joan and her mother and leading me into the kitchen. She indicated a place at the table. "Sit down. Sit down," she encouraged, bustling about and setting a plate before me.

She handed me a jar. "My homemade kosher dill pickles," she said. "Try one . . . you'll like it."

I crunched into the crispiest, most tasty pickle of my life. "Mmmm . . . delicious!" I exclaimed.

She glowed with pleasure, then turned to a steaming pot on the stove and ladled me a large bowl of chicken soup. It was chicken soup such as I had never tasted, and I told her so. She sat across from me and watched me eat.

"This is *excellent!*" I declared as I finished my first bowl and started on the refill she quickly set before me. With the second bowl she served me a plate of *latkas*. In answer to my unasked question, she chuckled. "Good Jewish food, *latkas* . . . potato pancakes . . . eat, eat."

So I ate—and ate. I couldn't remember tasting food such as this before. Another serving appeared. "Cheese *blintzes,*" she said. And while I enjoyed Jewish cuisine, she chatted about her favorite subject: her granddaughter. My mouth full most of the time, I couldn't say much, but I did smile and nod. Joan was also *my* favorite topic of conversation.

"What a girl she is!" she exclaimed. "A wonderful soul! She will someday make such a wonderful wife for a man."

I paused, a bite halfway to my mouth, trying to detect any notes of disapproval. But I could discern neither approval nor disapproval of myself as that husband for Joan, though she quite obviously approved of my appetite.

"Tomorrow is Passover," she informed me, and I nodded.

"Yes," I managed to say with a full mouth.

"Do you know about Passover?"

I nodded.

"And the seder dinner?"

My recent "Jewish" research had prepared me. I was fairly well informed about the Jewish holidays. I shared with her my knowledge of the event, adding, "And it's a very great privilege to be invited."

About that time Joan and her mother wandered into the kitchen. Grandmother cast a glance at me as I crunched into my fourth or fifth kosher dill, took Joan by the elbow, and guided her from the room. As Joan left, she looked back at me, paling perceptibly. I smiled and winked.

They were gone from the room so long that my confidence began to evaporate, and I was once again feeling nervous and apprehensive. But when Joan and her grandmother finally appeared, their faces wreathed in smiles, I relaxed. Joan leaned over the table and kissed me on the cheek, and I knew I'd been approved.

I was also stuffed.

The moment we got in the car to return to Westwood, Bess said, "Joan, what did Mother tell you?"

"Yes," I said. "I'm dying to hear it."

Joan's laugh was delightful to hear. Mimicking her grandmother's accent and pose perfectly, she repeated the woman's bans about dating Gentiles. She then concluded with, "Joanie, I *like* him. Him you can see. Joanie, *him* you can see!"

I took Joan's hand and squeezed it contentedly. Her response was a radiant smile, a portent of many years of happiness.

After our meeting with Grandmother, the seder was almost anticlimactic. Instead of the somber meal I had expected, with Joan's many aunts, uncles, and cousins present, along with Bess and Grandmother, the seder was a joyous, almost boisterous affair. Commemorating the Jews' exodus from Egyptian servitude, the event was celebrated with feasting, songs of celebration, and the detailed account of that deliverance.

Though the event was of great interest to me, mostly

because of my relationship with Joan, much of the symbolism was naturally lost on me. But after the seder was over, the question that had plagued me for weeks was answered. Both Joan and I also had much to celebrate: I had been accepted!

4

AN ENGINEERING VICTORY

After some deliberation, we set the wedding date for August 1964, just prior to the beginning of my second semester. We were married on August 15, in a simple, nonreligious ceremony—no rabbi, no priest—with a justice of the peace officiating, in the Little Chapel by the Sea at the Highlands Inn in Carmel, California.

Carmel is a picturesque little town midway between northern and southern California, a geographical fact that made it possible for Joan's family from Los Angeles and mine from the northern part of the state to be present. It was a lovely wedding, and Joan had never looked more beautiful. We spent a brief honeymoon at the Highlands Inn, marveling at our love for one another and enjoying Carmel's wind-shaped cypresses and windswept beach.

Among our wedding pictures were the last ones to be taken of my father. He died of a congenital heart defect just a month after our wedding. In a few more days

Dad would have enjoyed his forty-first birthday. His passing left a void in my life I could scarcely bear.

Until Dad was gone I didn't realize how much I loved him and had depended upon him—for his love, his stability, and his approval. And now that he was suddenly wrenched from my life, it seemed that my primary reason for living had been taken away. It took many difficult months for the wound to heal. I would often lie in bed at night and cry like a baby.

"Why," I asked no one in particular, because I didn't believe there was a God, "did such a good man as my father have to die so young? It's unfair. Unfair!" As my bride comforted me and helped ease my pain, we grew very close together, and gradually my purpose for living shifted from my father to my wife and mother, and later to my children.

Despite my pain and loss, I realized that my first priority must be the concentration of all my faculties upon my classes as I entered my final semester at the university. Now that I was married, I threw myself into my studies with abandon, reasoning that the straight A's I was making would enable me to finish strong and give me a better opportunity for a position.

It seemed that about every technical company in the country was seeking senior engineers, and I signed up to interview with a number of them. However, my best job offer actually came about through an unexpected source.

During my final semester, all UC Berkeley senior mechanical engineering students were required to take a course called "Engineering Laboratory," which was so difficult that if it had not been the last hurdle between them and graduation, many would have chosen another major. Three or four students, working as a team, are required to conduct laboratory tests on a wide variety of equipment, from gas turbines to computer-controlled robots.

This one class not only required the mastery of the cumulative knowledge of all other course work completed to that point, but it demanded that all participants learn the importance of functioning as a team, a vital key to engineering success.

Each week our team had three *concurrent* experiments going. The first involved planning, working out the theory of operation for a particular device, and designing a test procedure with time lines detailing the function of each team member during the following week's test, including all data sheets to be filled in during the test.

The second was an experiment we would conduct during a three-to-four-hour laboratory period, under the observation of a professor who would grade us on our ability to stick to the procedure time lines and how well we worked as a team. During the same week—the third of our concurrent assignments—we would analyze the data from the previous week's experiment, producing the graphs, tables, and analytical results that had been assigned or requested at the outset.

The work could be divided up any way we desired, but all team members received the same grade—whatever the test plan, or experiment, or data analysis we judged. Each experiment called for about 100 pages of planning, with another 100 pages of analysis. Neatness, accuracy, and timeliness were all computed into the final grade.

But the requirement that stared us in the face continually was the fact that our grade would be reduced one full letter *for every five minutes* it was late!

So grueling were these requirements that past years of students had determined that four men, working a full week (sometimes including nights and weekends), could just barely get the reports in on schedule.

We had a great team. Two of us were married, so we alternated work locations, and our wives would help us by keeping lots of hot, black coffee available, as well as an occasional meal. Often we spent the last two or three days working around the clock to complete our assignments. One fellow owned a twelve-digit mechanical calculator (this was the age of slide rules, before the pocket calculator), so he was given the heavy-duty data reduction task.

Each of us had a specialty which we contributed to the joint effort. We worked well together—well and long. But all of our hard work and long hours paid off, and we became the only team to get As on every single experiment during the thirteen-week semester.

On one experiment we were asked to measure several characteristics of a Mariner spacecraft simulator that had been donated to the university by the Jet Propulsion Laboratory (JPL) in Pasadena. The simulator consisted of a large block of metal which simulated the mass of the spacecraft, on which was mounted a Reaction Control System (RCS). The RCS was made up of a pressure tank and many tiny gas jets which would cause the spacecraft to turn in various directions.

The spacecraft was mounted on a spherical air bearing, a large, highly polished ball with a thin film of air flowing over it. In the center of the spacecraft was a sun sensor. By simulating the sun with a movie light, the sun sensor would cause the spacecraft RCS to align the spacecraft to the sun.

Our assignment was to generate a mathematical model of the way the spacecraft worked.

Traditionally, students had done this by measuring the reaction of the system by making periodic measurements with an alignment telescope called a theodolite. This procedure was slow and prone to error. Our team decided there must be a better way to solve the problem.

So we team-analyzed the problem, after which I came up with a way to use an old computer and automate the data acquisition. I sketched the idea and took it to the professor. He listened patiently and liked the idea.

"Okay," he said, "you've got my permission. However, you'll still have to maintain the same experiment schedule."

"Yes, I understand."

"You can use the machine shop," he went on, "but you'll have to buy your own materials."

"That's fair," I said. "We'll do it!"

I reported the matter to the group and began constructing a simple sensor system, using a section of a plastic sphere with a grid of lines on it, similar to the latitude and longitude lines on a globe. I machined grooves in this spherical piece and filled them with a black grease pencil. I put a light source inside the spherical grid and a stationary sensor on the outside, then mounted it on the spacecraft simulator. Now it was ready.

As the sphere rotated, the sensor registered a blip each time a grid line passed between it and the light source. The sensor blips were fed into the computer, which timed the blips and computed the data. The system worked beautifully. And with it we not only met the schedule, but saved ourselves a lot of test time.

The professor was impressed and offered to pay my annual student membership dues for the ASME (American Society of Mechanical Engineers) if I would write a paper on the little device and, assuming it was accepted, present it at the upcoming ASME Student Paper Contest. I was, of course, delighted to accept his offer. I wrote and submitted the paper, which was accepted.

Now the pressure was on. I made two practice presentations to the professor and his colleagues, who gave me a number of suggestions for its improvement. Then, to supplement the paper, I prepared some slides and a short film showing the system in operation.

The contest was being held at the University of Nevada at Reno, and the professor was to pick me up early in the morning of the contest day. At that time I didn't own a suit of my own, but I did have a couple of my father's that I'd fallen heir to. So I hurriedly grabbed one of them from the closet, along with a tie, kissed Joan good-bye, and dashed to the car. Three other students were going with us, as much to gamble in the casinos as to support my presentation.

As we drove along the freeway, the professor briefed me on the contest rules. He told me that the judges were professional engineers and teachers from all over the country. By this time I was getting nervous.

Then he said something that *really* made me nervous. He said, "Carman, you understand that this paper could be important to your future, don't you?"

"Yes, sir."

"You've got a good story, but it's much too long."

"Too long?"

"That's right. The rules say that you have exactly fifteen minutes for your presentation. And if you are even *one second* over fifteen minutes you'll be disqualified."

I gulped. Each of my first presentations had been between twenty-five and thirty minutes. I had to cut that in half.

"So," he went on, "I suggest you use the time between here and Reno to edit and practice that presentation. Okay?"

"Yes, sir, I understand," I said.

So, all the way to Reno, while my fellow passengers enjoyed the ride and the scenery, I edited, polished, and practiced my presentation, finally getting it down to slightly under the required fifteen minutes.

"I've got a suggestion," one of the students said. "Doing this in the car and on the stage are two different things. So I suggest that I signal you when you're down to the final thirty seconds. I'll signal you like this. Okay?"

I agreed, helpful for any support.

We arrived at the campus about ten o'clock and located the conference site. My presentation was scheduled for the afternoon. That was good. It would give me time to watch some of the others. Just then the professor came running.

"Steve, can you go on right away?"

"But I'm scheduled for this afternoon!"

"One student has canceled. Can you make it?"

I nodded and rushed to the men's room and changed. Then I handed my slides and film to the projectionist and nervously took my place, awaiting my call to appear. Finally my paper was announced, and I stepped up to the podium and called for my first slide. As I pointed to the screen, I noticed that my coat sleeve was green. (I had intended to wear Dad's *blue* suit.) Temporarily stunned, I glanced down at my pants. They were blue! *How awful I must look!*

I soon regained my composure. But realizing the brevity of time, I hurried through the first few slides. I glanced down at my friends in the front row now and then. Since they showed no evidence of alarm, I figured I was pretty much on schedule.

Then something happened that I hadn't counted on. When the projectionist rolled the film, he also turned off the lights. Now I couldn't see the audience, and had no way of judging the time. The film ended, and the lights came on. I saw my friends frantically waving their arms and giving me the "cut" sign. I rushed through one more sentence, concluded abruptly, and sat down with mere seconds to go.

I was positive that my funny clothes and poor presentation had lost me the contest. To my surprise, I received Honorable Mention. One of the engineering professors thanked me and said, "I think your presentation would be appropriate for the AIAA Student Paper Contest in Los Angeles. Why don't you enter it?"

I thanked him and did enter my paper. Again I was accepted, quite impressed by the title of the organization—The American Institute of Aeronautics and Astronautics—but not too sure what it was all about.

This time I was ready. I polished the paper, and *very carefully* packed my suitcase. I took my prepaid flight ticket and my hotel reservation (also prepaid), and flew to Los Angeles a day ahead of schedule. I was determined that nothing would go wrong this time!

I gave it my best. And this time my paper placed second, earning me several prizes, including a slide rule and a check for $100. (Wouldn't Joan be proud!)

But even more importantly, that exposure resulted in employment offers from eight different aerospace companies. Some even approached me at the conference. Besides, I was given a "red carpet" tour of JPL's Test and Research Facilities in Pasadena, the plant that had given us the Mariner spacecraft simulator.

By the time I had graduated, I had toured the facilities of most of the eight companies that had made me an offer. One of the best came from Texas Instruments in Richardson, Texas, near Dallas, where I would have been involved in designing assembly-line equipment. I rejected their offer because I wanted to stay closer to home, to be near mother and brother, as well as Joan's family.

After much deliberation, I accepted the offer from North American Aviation, Space Division, in Downey. There I was to be involved in a new space project called "Apollo," with the purpose of putting a man on the moon!

5

THE APOLLO PROJECT

I was eager to do well, to make a good first impression, which is probably the case with any new employee. But I suppose I felt an even heavier responsibility. Since my father's death the year before, I felt that Mom, who was unwell, and my brother, who was still in college, might become somewhat dependent upon me.

When I arrived at Downey, I learned that my January graduation had started me off on the wrong foot, so to speak, since all training courses for Apollo were designed to begin in July, when the June graduates arrived. This meant that I was already "out of phase" with the rest of my fellow, newly-hired engineers.

My desk was only one of several hundred in a huge bay of desks, all in single-file rows, with a supervisor's desk at the head of each row, separated for some privacy by five-foot-high partitions. During most of the day I was alone with one or two other January grads in this sea of desks. My assignment was to read a stack of material about Apollo and its various subsystems in preparation for the training sessions, which were not to begin until July.

I tried to appear studious, but the prospect of doing nothing but read for the next five months worried me. I told Joan, "This isn't my idea of a job on a 'fast-paced, high-pressure' space project." Of course she was sympathetic, but could do nothing about it.

When there was something in the reading material that I didn't understand, I would ask my supervisor an occasional question. Since most of the engineers were real "space nuts," who were well-acquainted with the history of the space program, and the supervisors themselves were former test pilots or military aircraft engineers, my questions must have exposed my ignorance about Apollo and the total space program.

After a few days of continuous reading, my supervisor beckoned. "Carman, put your reading material away. Grab a notebook and come with me."

I was on my feet in a moment, ready for action. He led me into a small conference room where I met two design engineers and a manufacturing foreman. The meeting dealt with the importance of vibration-testing all space program hardware, to verify if it could withstand the dynamics of launch—the pulsations of the launch vehicle rockets and the buffetings of the atmosphere which would cause the payload to shake or vibrate with great force.

My supervisor told the four of us—the two design engineers, the manufacturing foreman, and me—that we had been given the assignment to design and build a vibration test facility capable of "shaking" the Apollo command and service modules, either separately or stacked together, so as to simulate the vibration effects of launch.

My personal task was threefold: to write procedures for the installation of the command and service modules on the test fixture, to write the procedures for performing the test, and then to conduct the tests when the hardware was ready. Now I had an engineering task worthy of my interest. And from that day on I was rarely at my desk.

I immersed myself in the task: I studied the Apollo command and service module drawings, concentrating especially on those dealing with the mounting details. I also studied the design drawings of the mammoth vibration fixture. The fixture consisted of a massive ring about twenty feet in diameter that was mounted on four tall columns or "legs." In use, the Apollo command and service module would fit into the ring with its base about ten or twelve feet above the floor. This permitted the rocket motor nozzle extension, which hung beneath the service module, to clear the floor.

I also studied the operating manuals of the large electrodynamic shaker system. Three of these systems were mounted on columns and attached to the mounting ring. To simulate various modes of vibration, the three shakers could be operated either separately or in unison. After several months of development, the facility and the procedures were finished and ready for testing, which was performed at one end of the large clean room where the Apollo spacecrafts were assembled.

In use, the noise echoed from the polished walls of the clean room with such volume and intensity that all personnel were required to leave the site prior to each test. The few of us involved in the testing wore special ear protection. We never did achieve full launch simulation test levels, because the noise was so loud—even at one-fortieth of the launch level—that it was disturbing to the residents in the surrounding neighborhood.

Because of this, the vibration tests were discontinued after obtaining the basic response data needed to verify the design. Nevertheless, the vibration testing went well, and my procedures received praise from the supervisors.

During the tests, I wore special ear protectors and stood directly beneath the service module, alongside the large, bellshaped rocket nozzle to check for leaks in the fluid-filled tanks and plumbing. The tanks had been filled with water or Freon (a cleaning fluid) and pressurized to simulate the mass of rocket fuel which they would carry at launch. This testing was critically important, and even a small leak could mean trouble, because this full load of fuel would be needed to propel the command and service module from the moon back to the earth.

During one of the tests, I saw a small spot of liquid on the floor directly below the service module. It appeared to be just a tiny drip, but even that could prove disastrous; so I hit the "Stop" button. Everybody came running from the control room.

"What's the matter, Steve?"

I pointed. "We've got a leak somewhere. Let's check it out."

They brought tall ladders and checked out the module. Interestingly, there were no valves or joints in the plumbing and tanks directly above the drip on the floor. "Maybe it was blown there from another spot," I said. "Look some more."

So they moved the ladders again. As they did, I saw

another drip. They moved again and checked again and found nothing. By this time there was quite a crowd forming, but nobody could find the source of a drip or leak. I was puzzled. That moisture was coming from somewhere, and we had to find it. I moved back away from beneath the service module to think—and as I did, I saw another drip on the floor.

"C'mon, Carman," one of the men said, "what's going on?"

"I don't know," I said, "but you can see for yourself that there's a drip." I was beginning to wonder if the fire sprinkler in the ceiling of the high bay was dripping.

"But that drip's not even under the module!" someone noted.

Just then a mechanic noticed that my white, clean room smock had a wet spot on it. And even as he watched, he observed a drip fall from my hard hat to that very spot on my smock.

"Hey, look!" he shouted triumphantly. "The drips are coming from Steve's ear protectors!"

It was true. I had removed my fluid-filled ear protectors and clamped them out of the way on top of my hard hat. Somehow the protectors had developed a slight leak, and the fluid had dripped on the floor. Naturally, as I moved about, the drips followed me. So I was the culprit, and there were no leaks in the service module. But we all had a good laugh at my expense, and the problem was solved.

With the completion of the vibration tests, I found myself still out of sync with the regular training classes. So I began attending a special class on the installation and testing of pyrotechnics. The particular pyrotechnics I was being schooled in had to do with the little

51

"arming" devices used to ignite and "fire" or "launch" certain spacecraft equipment. These explosives ranged in size from tiny separation devices to the solid rocket booster motor used in the launch escape system.

This particular class was specifically designed to teach the development and testing of the parachutes used to lower the command module safely to earth after its reentry into the earth's atmosphere. The stowing and release system for these parachutes was extremely sophisticated. These parachutes, which were stowed in the "top deck" compartment, at the pointed end of the gumdrop-shaped command module, were deployed (released) by a carefully sequenced series of pyrotechnic events.

First, the nose cone part of the heat shield was ejected with high-pressure thrusters, and a small parachute would be fired from a mortar to carry the heat shield away from the command module. Then two medium-size drogue chutes would fire from large mortars to deploy and stabilize the command module. Perfectly in sequence, three small mortars would then fire to deploy pilot parachutes, each of which would pull one of the three huge main parachutes from its compartment.

Then again, at splashdown, the main chutes would be separated from the command module by an explosive cutter to prevent the heavy wet chutes from dragging the command module under the water. As sophisticated and complex as these events were, they were not the really tough part of the parachute assignment. The most critical task was the testing and installation of the three main parachutes.

The task of installing the three football-field-size parachutes and installing each in its fitted sector of the command module was a critical one. The total time for this exacting procedure could not exceed fifteen minutes or the parachute would absorb so much air that it could not be forced into its tiny, precisely designed space.

There were two possible dangers I had to be aware of. First, if we exceeded our fifteen-minute installation time, the parachute would expand and exceed its predesigned space on the top deck of the command module, which would place it too close to the heat shield. If this happened, the heat generated by reentry speeds of over 25,000 miles per hour would melt holes in the parachute. Second, if any knot was improperly tied, the parachute might not open causing the command module to impact the water too hard.

It was truly a time-pressured task. But with the help of the super team from the parachute manufacturer, we did it.

After the parachute procedures were under control, I was assigned the tasks of writing procedures for installing the heat shield, the crew couches, and most of the equipment in the crew compartment. Following this came writing the weight and balance procedures used to locate the center of gravity of the command and service modules; the procedures for tumble-cleaning both modules; and the procedures for the alignment of the modules to one another.

Finally . . . I again began the series of Apollo familiarization training courses. But this time another hindrance came to light: I was by now overqualified for the training.

All of my firsthand experience with the vehicles had left me more knowledgeable than most instructors. So, after attending each course for a few days, I would request permission to take the final exam, with the idea that if I passed it, I would forego the remainder of the class. As a result, I attended very few classes and returned to work.

My familiarity with Apollo's many subsystems resulted in my initial assignment to the Cape Kennedy launch site. Apollo spacecraft number 009 was scheduled to test its heat shield with an unmanned reentry, using robotlike boxes to simulate crew switch manipulations, and I was selected as a part of this first unmanned launch team. Joan and Scott, our baby son, went with me.

Scott, our first child, had been born in the spring of 1965. His middle name was Donald, after my father. Scott was a delight to us, a happy and healthy baby we were proud to show off. I knew Dad would have loved him. But as it was, Dad never even knew that his first grandchild was on the way.

Now and then I would ponder a statement I had heard my uncle make—about those who had died being able to look down from "heaven" and see their loved ones. I would have liked to believe that this was so, and that Dad would thus have the privilege of observing his grandchild. But I knew this was foolishness; so I dismissed the thought from my mind.

About two months after Scott was born, we drove to San Francisco to visit my mother. She was delighted with Scott, and some of my favorite memories of Mom are of her bouncing Scott upon her knees. Though Mom was a young grandmother, just forty when Scott was born, she looked much older than her years. Like one of her sisters, Mom had required a daily insulin shot, which had taken its toll on her body.

Shortly after our visit with Mom, we were awakened at four o'clock one morning by the telephone. Half asleep, I fumbled the phone to my ear. "Hello . . ."

"Is that you, Steve?"

"Yes . . ."

"This is Judy . . . Aunt Judy . . ."

Instantly I was wide awake, sensing an emergency of some kind. "Yes. Yes, Aunt Judy. What's up?"

"It's your mother, Steve. . . ."

"Mother? Is something wrong?"

"Yes, Steve . . . the doctor says . . . he says she might not make it." There was a catch in her voice. "Can you come up here . . . right away?"

"Yes . . . sure," I said, my mind reeling with the news, "as soon as we can catch a plane. But what happened? Was she in an accident or something?"

Aunt Judy's voice was stronger now. "No, she was feeling fine, going to work every day as usual. Then she suddenly passed out yesterday. . . ."

I knew that Mom had recently undergone intestinal surgery and asked if this emergency was in some way related to that. "The doctor thinks it might be related," Judy said. "Anyway, Steve, get here as quickly as you can. Okay?"

"Okay, Aunt Judy. I'll make flight reservations and call you back to let you know when we'll arrive."

"We'll pick you up at the airport, Steve. Good-bye."

When I hung up, I realized I was shaking. Joan was fully awake by now, and I told her what I'd heard. We hugged each other for a moment. Could this really be happening? I wondered. How desperately I wanted to believe that Mom would pull through this crisis. Or at least until I arrived.

We hurriedly made our preparations, left Scott with Joan's mother, and rushed to the airport. Neither of us said much during the hour-long flight to San Francisco.

My Uncle Al met us at the airport, and we quickly transferred our luggage to his car and headed for the hospital.

"Your brother's at the hospital," Uncle Al volunteered. "He came over from Berkeley a couple of hours ago." I was relieved, glad that somebody had called him.

"How's Mom doing?" I asked, almost afraid of the answer.

Uncle Al shook his head. "Not so good, Steve. She seems to be slipping fast."

Al drove as fast as possible, but it seemed like a terribly long time before we arrived at the hospital. When we got to Mom's room, my brother, Aunt Judy, and a man in a priest's garb were standing outside the closed door.

"Can we go in?" I asked.

At that moment a nurse came out of the room. She heard my question. "Are you the other son?" I nodded, hardly trusting my voice to speak. Without a word she took my hand and Donald's hand and led us into the room, to the side of Mom's bed.

I was shocked at Mom's appearance. She seemed to have aged years during the few weeks since we'd seen her. Tubes and wires and intravenous solution bottles were hooked to her, which served to emphasize her apparently critical condition. At first I thought she had already died, but the slow, rhythmic rise and fall of her chest reassured me that she was still breathing.

I picked up Mom's hand. It seemed no larger than a child's, pitifully tiny and thin. I squeezed the hand that had so recently fondled her first grandchild. There was no response. Tears rolled down my cheeks, but I didn't feel them.

The nurse said, "I think she can still hear, if you

shout." At that she placed her mouth close to Mom's ear and shouted, "Mrs. Carman, your sons are here! Your sons are here!"

For a long moment there was no response. Then, ever so slowly, Mom began to stir. Her head rotated in our direction, and she struggled to open her eyes. Finally she was able to open them for a few seconds. Her tired eyes searched for and finally focused on the faces of her sons, then closed heavily.

I thought I saw a faint smile of recognition. Suddenly, seeing my mother like this was more than I could bear. I choked and began to cry, and hurriedly left the room.

In the hallway Joan helped me compose myself. "Go back, Steve," she said. "Hold your mother's hand. She needs you."

The uninvited priest introduced himself. He seemed nice enough, but his presence seemed irrelevant, an intrusion. I wondered why he had come, who had sent him. He said, "Isn't it amazing how the body holds on to life . . . ?"

I didn't answer him, and wished he would leave. I looked at Aunt Judy, who had been silently weeping, as though to ask her, Why is he here? But she looked away.

Joan went with me back into the room, and I picked up my mother's thin hand again and looked down at her pale, drawn face. In that long moment, I knew. I knew that even as I had lost my father, I was about to lose my mother. The thought was almost more than I could bear.

Soon I was weeping almost uncontrollably again.

Why was death so awful? I had no answers.

The doctor came in and asked everyone to leave the

room. When he came out, in answer to my unasked question, he said, "As you know, Mrs. Carman underwent surgery a few weeks ago, and a portion of her intestines was removed. She seemed to be doing well. But apparently peritonitis—inflammation of the lining of the intestinal cavity—has set in. She's very ill."

"Will she . . . is she . . ." I started, but could not finish the question.

His eyes were compassionate as he shook his head slowly. "She was about to expire when she arrived at the hospital. Most of her organs had already ceased to function." He paused. "I'm sorry, folks. It's just a matter of time. And not very much time. I'm sorry."

Two hours later my dear mother breathed her last. And I, the oldest son, was now in charge. It was more difficult than I can possibly tell. I had been responsible for most of my father's funeral arrangements, and I was now responsible for my mother's. After the funeral, it was up to me to handle the disposition of my parents' possessions. After everything had been distributed between my brother, my aunt and uncle, and myself, and the remainder of my mother's worldly goods sold, I inherited nearly $7,500 in unpaid bills.

I struggled for months to pay them off, working long hours of overtime on Apollo. About eight months after my mother's death, a long-forgotten insurance policy check arrived, followed soon by some funds from other sources. The bills were finally paid.

But my emotional loss took much longer to heal.

6

AT THE CAPE

It was good to get physically away from the recent stresses and to throw myself wholeheartedly into the Apollo project. Though there were many living conditions in Florida that Joan and I didn't particularly like, we managed very well. And all in all, our months there exerted a positive influence on our lives.

The Cape was very primitive at that time, and our apartment near the ocean in Cocoa Beach had to be routinely sprayed to keep the cockroach population under control. The green water that flowed from our faucets required boiling or heavy filtering to look drinkable, although the "locals" claimed it was safe.

After completing the subsystems testing, the Apollo command module was moved to the Pyrotechnic Installation Building (PIB), where the explosive charges and their initiators were to be installed, along with the parachutes.

I followed the spacecraft as it was moved to the PIB.

Encased in its protective covering, it was large and impressive. But as it was hauled slowly along the long, isolated road, with no other buildings or roadways in its vicinity, I had time to note just how remote and isolated the PIB was.

I realized that there was a very practical reason for this remoteness, and shivered at the thought: A sudden spark could ignite a rocket engine and destroy the entire plant. With no other buildings nearby, only the lives of those working in the PIB would be in jeopardy.

It seemed that I had barely dropped off to sleep that night when the phone rang in our little apartment. I was informed that "The parachute and pyro installation procedures are next. . . ."

Within minutes I was out of bed, quickly dressed, and into my car. But to my surprise the night road wasn't as smooth as it had been during the day. The headlights picked up hundreds of "sticks" strewn across the road, which made it very rough and bumpy to drive.

As I bumped along, I took a closer look at the sticks, and to my horror, they weren't sticks at all. They were snakes! The road was covered thickly with snakes, all kinds of them, including some that I strongly suspected were poisonous. Later I learned the reason: the hot daytime heated the road, and at night the cold-blooded snakes came out of the cooler swamp to warm their bodies on that still warm but little traveled stretch of highway.

For some reason running over them didn't seem to kill very many. It was the same every time I drove over that stretch of road during the night: covered with snakes!

The morning dawned before we finished the parachute installation, including the pyrotechnics and heat shield. On my way home I noted that the road was now clear of snakes. But I had made the mistake of leaving a car window rolled down during the night, and a family of tree frogs had moved in. I wondered if I should apply for hazardous duty pay.

After the successful launch and reentry of spacecraft 009, the Cape assignment ended and we headed back home to California, to be handed another exciting task. Because of my familiarity with most Apollo subsystem hardware, I had been selected to participate in crew training.

Although NASA had a team of specialist crew trainers, whose job it was to familiarize the astronauts with the actual operation of the system, my intimate knowledge of the command module had earned for me the opportunity—and heavy responsibility—of seeing that these crew members acquired a hands-on familiarity with the equipment in the crew compartment.

Then followed the months of intensive training of these men, during which time I became so intimately involved in their lives that when the tragic fire occurred and the three astronauts lost their lives, I was devastated.

After mulling all these events over in my mind for a while, I decided to look for another job. I reviewed my accomplishments on Apollo, completed my resumé, and took it with me to an interview I had set up with my friend Al Sivonen's father. I liked him immediately. He seemed to be just the kind of person I would like to work for: experienced, talented, clever. On top of that, he was very patient.

Mr. Sivonen introduced me to the small crew that worked for him in his development firm. After the mass of people I had been working with, the small size of this operation seemed like a plus to me. Mr. Sivonen showed me around the plant and showed me some of the mechanisms they were working on. Then he introduced me to the director of his division, who invited me into his office for the worst interview experience of my entire life.

To begin with, this engineer was a Stanford graduate, which was an immediate negative, since my degree was from UC Berkeley, and the two universities are rivals. And this "Stanford man" seemed bent on demonstrating his superiority.

I had scarcely entered the room and handed him my resumé when he said, "Go to the chalkboard and work out these problems for me."

Then he contrived problems covering motion of transmission gear trains, beam bending, and others, none of which I'd even thought about since graduation three years before. Needless to say, I fumbled around a bit in trying to answer them.

At that my interviewer said, "Carman, you've got to stay sharp in the engineering discipline . . . *Stanford* professors drilled this into us."

I was glad when the "interview" was over and I could go. I felt that there was absolutely no hope for this job. But to my surprise I got a call a few days later from Mr. Sivonen.

"Congratulations, Steve," he said. "You got the job."

"Thanks" was about all I could say, to cover my surprise. "When do you want me to begin?"

"Well, we're relocating the plant, so I can't give you a definite date."

Since I wasn't in a bind, I told him it was okay, and didn't give notice. But shortly after the plant was moved, I got a phone call. "Sorry, Steve, but the new facility is more expensive than we anticipated. We can't afford to hire you."

Before I could begin another search, I was contacted by an engineering search firm and was offered an interview with the Space Division of General Electric Company. After the initial interview in California, they flew Joan and me back to Philadelphia. We arrived with the springtime, and everything was in full bloom. We liked the area, and I was impressed by the company and the position they offered.

I accepted contingent to our remaining in California until our second child was born. When our daughter Sheri arrived in May 1967, I gave thirty days notice to North American, and my Apollo days were over.

On the day of our move, as the movers were loading our few belongings into the van, I was surprised to see Al, my supervisor, and Lloyd Mustin walk up the driveway. "We couldn't let you get away without giving you this," Al said, handing me a framed certificate.

"What is it?"

"You've been honored as Engineer of the Year."

I showed the plaque to Joan. She smiled. "I'm not surprised. You deserve it." And for a brief moment I wished that my parents could have known. How proud of me they would have been.

I thanked the two men and told them good-bye. It would be a number of years before I saw Lloyd Mustin again, under circumstances that would be surprising for both of us. We kept in contact for many years after this. Al and his wife later joined the Peace Corps, while Lloyd remained at Rockwell to work on several space projects which would occasionally bring us together again.

7

THE STORM

The first step in our cross-country move was to locate a place in which to live. Joan and I flew to Philadelphia in late May 1967, and after considerable searching located a small three-bedroom house in Ridley Park, a quaint community near the Delaware River. I expressed my concern to the realtor about the railroad track that ran behind the house.

He laughed. "No problem. It's only a spur that's rarely used," he said. "Just once a year to keep the weeds down."

After we'd signed the lease and were driving away, the train rumbled by. "Well, that's our yearly train disturbance," I said.

Joan gave me a dubious smile.

(The realtor was "somewhat" off in his predictions. As it turned out, instead of the "annual" use of the spur, we were jolted out of our chairs about three times a day. Of course, two-year-old Scott didn't mind. He'd rush to the window and wave at the engineer. It was a different thing, though, for our guests, who would nervously grip their chairs as the sound increased in intensity and we could no longer hear each other speak.)

Back in California, Joan and the two children moved in with her mother, while I drove our car across the country. They would fly and join me as soon as I arrived and the moving van had delivered our household goods.

En route to Pennsylvania I planned to visit a number of national parks, but the long, tedious hours of driving left me too tired to do any extra sightseeing. For the most part, the trip was long, dull, and boring, highlighted by an occasional good meal and my nightly progress-report telephone call to Joan.

One of those lonesome, boring nights afforded me some unexpected excitement. I had been on the road almost eight hours since leaving my hotel that morning somewhere in Wyoming when it began to rain so heavily that my windshield wipers could no longer keep the windshield clear. Since I was still forty miles short of my target destination for the night, I decided to pull into the very next motel available.

Shortly thereafter I saw signs directing me to a motel off the main highway. At the edge of this little community that seemed to be on the edge of nowhere, I saw a motel with a "no vacancy" sign. Surely, I thought, that must be a mistake. How could any motel this far off the main track be full?

I braved the rain and pushed my way into the motel lobby. "Sorry, sir," the kindly lady at the desk told me, "but we don't have a single room."

My face must have registered my bewilderment. "Are you sure?" I asked.

"Yes. And the other two motels in town are full too."

"They are?"

"Yes, it's because of the hunters."

"Hunters?" I responded blankly.

She looked at me more closely. "You're not a hunter?"

"No. Why?"

"Well, tomorrow's opening day for deer season. The town's full of hunters, ready for an early start in the morning. Are you *sure* you're not a hunter?" she asked again.

As I assured her I wasn't a hunter, I turned to leave.

"Wait a minute," she said. "I . . . I might be able to find you a place." She paused uncertainly. "And you don't have a gun?"

"That's right. No gun. Why?"

"Well, my mother sometimes lets out rooms at her home. But she won't rent to hunters. She hates guns."

"I don't like them either," I assured her, reminding her of my nonhunter status. She looked at me closely for another long moment, then went to the telephone. After a rather lengthy discussion, she turned to me. "My mother says it's okay."

She gave me directions to what was probably the last vacant room—and bed—in the whole town. I drove to the large farmhouse on the outskirts of town and stood in the rain until the kindly, elderly lady responded to my knock. She showed me the upstairs room with its old-fashioned, fourposter bed and apologized for the bathroom being "down the hall."

At that moment the room became as light as day with a flash of lightning, which was followed instantly by an ear-splitting roll of thunder. It startled us both.

My hostess frowned. "The good Lord must be angry about all those guns in town."

I searched her face for a hint of facetiousness in her remark, but there was none. Apparently she really thought that God had sent the thunder and lightning to harass the hunters. I smiled to myself, because I understood the cause and effect of certain atmospheric conditions that brought about such weather. But I didn't want to disillusion her belief that God was real, even though I knew he was not.

I changed the subject. "May I use your telephone to call my wife?" I asked. When the woman hesitated I said, "I'll call her collect. I call her every night I'm away from home."

She led me to her downstairs phone, where I had difficulty talking to Joan because of the stormy interference.

After talking to Joan I returned to my room and tried to sleep. But the frequency and violence of the thunder and lightning kept me awake. The power and brilliance of the brighter-than-sun lightning, and the violence of the cannonlike thunder that seemed to shake the house provided me with the most powerful electrical display I had ever seen. Unable to sleep, I watched the lightning's forked tongues flash from the low-lying storm clouds and strike other clouds and then the earth.

I thought of the landlady's words. "The good Lord must be angry tonight. . . ."

What a typical Midwestern statement, I thought. Out here in these isolated towns the people are so poorly educated that they still believe the ancient, outmoded idea of a Supreme Being who could get angry and cause stormy weather.

Utterly amazing! I thought. Especially since modern space-age meteorologists can provide the *scientific* explanation for rain and lightning and thunder. And yet so many people still think and talk of a God. Smugly I thought, *Someday science will so thoroughly explain all of these phenomena to future generations that they will recognize all of these man-made ideas about spiritual beings for what they are: mere rationalizations of primitive culture.*

Then I remembered the disturbing article I had recently read about one of the scientists I greatly respected for his contributions to the space program: Dr. Wernher von Braun, the genius rocketeer. The article indicated that Dr. von Braun had recently embraced Christianity. And the author quoted Dr. von Braun's response to questions concerning the impact of his new "religion" on his ideas of searching for life in space.

The article had told of Dr. von Braun's frank Christian stance, of how he now "professed a faith in Jesus Christ as his God and 'Savior.' (*A savior from what?* I wondered.) Such a statement from this eminent German-born scientist confused me. And I reasoned that this must be some sort of a government-initiated plan to appease and relax the opposition of the Bible-believers who argued against sending man into space.

I knew that scientists would never go along with such a sham. But then von Braun had seemed so sincere. . . .

I thought of the time Dr. von Braun had come to visit the Apollo project at North American. As he was being escorted into the high-bay clean room where I was working on the command module installation, I had stopped to listen to his conversation with the Apollo project manager, who was his tour guide. Though von

Braun was surrounded by a crowd of other scientists, I did manage to catch a glimpse of his stately features.

Then, as I almost held my breath in wonder, the great man paused directly in front of the spacecraft I was working on. And I could clearly hear his words as he asked detailed questions about how the umbilical between modules was separated prior to reentry. By the way he spoke I could tell that he was intimately familiar with the Apollo lunar mission plan.

And I had been proud to be a part of the same program to which this brilliant man had contributed so much in design and promotion. But now he was a Christian?

In the intermittent darkness and brilliance of my farm home bedroom, I distinctly remembered the reporter's questions—and von Braun's answers.

"As a Christian, Dr. von Braun," the reporter had asked, "you must have second thoughts about traveling into space to look for life, don't you? For if we find life out there, won't it mean that there is no God?"

"On the contrary . . ." The eminent scientist had responded in a way that had caused me to think very deeply. ". . . I am now more interested than ever before in a search for life in the universe, for if we find another civilization in space, I believe it would be the greatest proof of God's existence man has ever known. You see, I believe that God created the universe, *including man*. And if there are other beings in this universe, they exist only because God created them . . . and they would then know the same God that I know."

Dr. von Braun had talked about the possibility of a world where there was no "sin," a planet where men lived in harmony with God, "as he intended in his original creation."

70

Still fully awake in my bed I remembered my shock at von Braun's words. I couldn't believe the great man had said such things. Had he lost his mind? Yet he had seemed so intelligent. Perhaps he was growing old and getting to the point where he was slipping a bit as he began worrying about death. . . .

I don't remember what time it was when the storm finally dissipated enough for me to sleep. But I slept late the next day and awakened to bright sunshine streaming through the thin curtains.

8

PENNSYLVANIA DUTCH TREAT

A few days after my stormy night's experience, I arrived in the City of Brotherly Love and was rejoined the following day by Joan and the two children. I began work immediately in the Re-entry Systems Division of the General Electric Company in their test facilities, which were housed at that time in a converted warehouse on Chestnut Street in Philadelphia.

Though I normally rode the commuter train from Ridley Park to Union Station, then walked the few blocks from the terminal to my office, I did ride for a while with Tom Harkins, one of the technicians I worked with.

During those commuter rides, we talked about a number of things. One day Tom asked, "What church do you attend?"

For an answer, I launched into my usual statement to the effect that "Religion's a necessity only for those who feel a need for something beyond the scientific view of the world,"concluding with, "And personally I've never felt that need."

Tom listened carefully to my philosophy, then spoke of his Catholic upbringing. He admitted, though, that "I've always had some doubts. . . ."

As time went on, Tom stopped attending church altogether and adopted my atheistic attitudes, as did many of those around me. I was never antagonistic to religious people, believing as I did in a "live and let live" policy. But when I was asked about my position, I was so convinced of my point of view, and so articulate in stating that point of view, that I could make it sound so perfectly rational that it would appear to be ridiculous to subscribe to any other line of thinking.

At the time I started working with GE's Re-entry Systems Division, GE's Space Division was working on a NASA contract for the Manned Orbiting Laboratory (MOL) project, which was a precursor to Skylab. Portions of the MOL were under test at the Re-entry Systems Division, and I was assigned the task of testing some torque motors designed for use in driving the rotation of solar panels on the MOL.

The manufacturer of these high-torque, low-speed (as low as one revolution per hour) motors had no equipment sensitive enough to test them. So I was given six weeks in which to design and complete a test of the "cogging" or "torque ripple" of these motors.

Using a precision rate table and a video camera which tracked the ripple in the motion of the motor, I successfully completed the test within the allotted time. Although the test revealed that the motor was unacceptable for MOL's use, my findings precipitated another series of tests. These further tests, in addition to extending the contract several more months, also resulted in improved motor design, and advanced the state of the art in this type of measurement.

I was personally rewarded by being promoted to supervisor of a new development laboratory.

This new assignment was a dream job, and I found myself eager to get to work each day. I often stayed at my office late into the night doing what engineers love to do: dream up new applications for advanced technology, then design and build the hardware to put the ideas into practice. To do this I was provided with everything I needed. I was given a large budget with which to procure special lab equipment. I had a staff of machinists in a small, well-equipped machine shop, and an electronics shop capable of printed circuit board fabrications and component assembly.

On top of that—which put the frosting on the cake—I was "required" to travel to conferences covering the latest in new technology (lasers, computers, etc.), anything that might have a possible application for the manufacturing and testing of spacecraft at GE.

In addition to my own lab work, I was also responsible for the production of development hardware for some of the scientists in other GE laboratories.

During my eighteen months as supervisor and chief design engineer for the development lab, I was involved with the designing of a number of very interesting projects—for example, the automated machine that determined the weight, center of gravity, moments, and products of inertia with a single setup, which reduced test time from days to minutes. I also designed the electronics to go with this equipment, thus adding to my mechanical design background. I designed a data acquisition system, which utilized the central, time-share computer.

I designed a portable system for detecting explosive gases, such as hydrogen, which tend to collect in pockets in the ceilings of clean rooms where the gas is used. I did extensive work with a laser to evaluate its use as a surface roughness detector. All of this, and much more, using the very latest in newly developed technology and equipment, kept my professional life perpetually interesting.

But while I was having the time of my life, Joan was becoming less and less satisfied at home. The four-season climate left her freezing in the cold, snowy winter—afraid to travel on the icy roads—and sweltering in the hot, humid, mosquito-infested summer.

The "once-a-year train" succeeded in awakening our children from their daily naps. The curious but stand-offish neighbors increased her loneliness. On top of all this, the fact that she had neither family nor friends to fellowship with made Pennsylvania life "the pits" as far as Joan was concerned. Despite all this, Joan put up with the discomforts and stuck with me because I was so happy with my work.

Our life in Pennsylvania hadn't been totally devoid of enjoyable times, though there hadn't been too many of them. We had enjoyed our summertime visits to the little park by the lake in Ridley Park. We all enjoyed the fresh air, and the kids liked the playground. Scott loved to play on the swings and the monkey bars.

On one of those days in the park we had a good laugh at our little girl's expense. Sheri was just learning to walk that summer. She was excited about her mobility and explored everything. But she went a little too far when she followed a duck into the water. The look of surprise on her face when she discovered she couldn't walk on the water was precious to behold.

Occasionally Joan and I would get a baby-sitter and take a train into Philadelphia to shop, or to New York to see a play. We especially loved the beautiful Pocono Mountains and the colorful leaves displayed by the fall trees. And we did enjoy driving around in the Pennsylvania Dutch country. We discovered a large Amish family named Carman (the same spelling as my name) and wondered if my ancestors could have been Amish.

Joan enrolled in a sewing class, doing so well in the beginning class that she moved on to the advanced. Not to be outdone, I enrolled in a beginner's guitar class and learned to play simple tunes. I had so much fun with my guitar that Joan also took lessons.

Still, it was probably sheer boredom that prompted Joan to ask one of the neighbors if she and the kids could go to church with them. Early in our courtship Joan and I had discussed our religious differences, and she had agreed with my position, which I had adopted from my father: "If you and the kids ever want a religion, you can select one to suit your needs. But it's not for me."

I had never doubted the fact that there must be some social benefit to be gained from religion—"like there is with any other 'club'"—but I could never understand why people would ritually spend Sundays in church, worshiping the idea that man was somehow inferior to a Supreme Being.

Joan knew full well my thoughts on church, and knew better than to try and coax me to go to church with her. So the following Sunday, while I busied myself with things around the house, she and the kids walked to a nearby church with the neighbors. It proved to be an unforgettable day.

When Joan returned home, changed her clothes, and

began preparing dinner, I could tell that she was agitated and upset. I asked her, "Is something bothering you?"

She shook her head, but wouldn't talk. Joan was like that. Whenever she was hurt or frightened, she became quiet and refused to talk. When she clammed up like that, I usually reacted by getting angry, which didn't help. Joan would then begin crying, and I'd throw things or stomp out the door to go for a drive or walk to calm myself down.

This time, it was while I was well into my standard speech on the importance of communication in marriage when Joan finally spoke.

Struggling to hold back the tears, she said, "Steve, it was awful! Just awful!"

Her obvious distress melted my anger. I moved to her side and put my arm around her. "What happened? Tell me."

"Well, we got to church and sat down. Then the people sang some songs—I didn't know any of them—and then the preacher got up. He started telling a story in the New Testament about how Jesus was killed, *crucified*. . . . And then he said . . ."

At that Joan started to cry and could hardly get the words out. "He said . . . well, he said that . . . that the Jews . . . that the Jews killed Jesus! That's what he said."

Not knowing what else to do, I put both arms around her and drew her closer, trying to comfort her.

"I got scared . . . very scared! I was afraid that they'd find out that I'm a Jew and . . . I don't know what I thought they might do."

She looked up at me. "Was that right, Steve? *Did* the Jews kill Jesus? Did they?"

Her question surprised me. "I don't know." I was startled that she would even ask. She knew my thoughts about the Bible, how I considered it to be just stories—fables would be more accurate—that had been written by religious zealots long ago who'd been intent upon promoting their own brand of religion.

"I don't know," I said again, "but you're the one with the religious background. What were you taught about this man they called Jesus?"

She thought for a moment. "Only that he was a teacher, a good teacher. But we were mostly warned that the Gentiles would try to convince us Jews that Jesus was the Messiah . . . or that he was God. I expected to hear that much about him in this church—but not that Jews were the ones who killed him."

"Maybe that's just the preacher's point of view," I said, not knowing what else to say.

Apparently feeling somewhat better by now, Joan hugged me, then went about her business of preparing lunch.

While she did, I was thinking about how this incident simply confirmed my atheistic beliefs: these people were no better than anybody else, maybe even worse, because anybody who believed that "God stuff" had to be a bit demented. It was just like Dad had said: "Religion's got nothing in it for me."

Joan looked up from the stove. "Steve, if that's Christianity, I don't ever want to have anything more to do with church. Never again!"

"That's fine with me," I agreed, trying hard not to have my words sound like "I told you so."

True to her word, Joan never again mentioned that experience as long as we lived in Pennsylvania.

In the spring of 1969, we received a letter from

Joan's younger brother, inviting us to his wedding. Realizing that Joan could really use a break from her monotonous routine, and that it was financially impossible for all of us to fly to California to the wedding, I volunteered to stay home with the kids while she flew to the wedding.

That choice set in motion a chain of events that brought great changes to our lives.

Joan thoroughly enjoyed the wedding, as well as her visit with her mother and many old friends and neighbors. She learned that one couple we'd been good friends with had moved to Denver, and decided to stop over and visit them on the way home. When Joan called me from Denver, I couldn't recall hearing her so excited for a long, long time.

"I love it here, Steve," she said. "Everything about it. The Rockies. And Denver. It feels so much like home. I like it so much better than the Northeast."

"I'm glad you're enjoying yourself," I said, warming to her obvious enthusiasm.

"Steve . . . Steve . . . I've been wondering," she began. "Do you think it's possible that we might move to Denver?"

I took a deep breath. I'd been thinking a lot about our situation in Ridley Park since Joan had been gone, realizing that the only joy we had was in my work. Scott and Sheri were still very young and weren't in school yet. It would be no problem for them if we moved. But where could I ever find another dream job like the one I had with GE?

Despite that question, I'd even thought about contacting the Engineering Search Bureau, the organization that had introduced me to GE. And for some reason I couldn't at that time analyze, I'd kept their business card in my wallet.

Talking now with Joan, I suddenly remembered: Engineering Search Bureau's office was based in Denver. Coincidental?

I told Joan all this and gave her the Bureau's phone number. "Why don't you phone them and see if there are any engineering opportunities in the Denver area."

"Okay, I'll do it." The lilt in her voice was beautiful to my ears. "I'll call you back tomorrow."

The next day the lilt in her voice was still there when she called me. "Steve, the Engineering Search people told me that the Martin Company has just won a big NASA contract to build the spacecraft that's going to land on Mars. And *they need a lot of engineers.*"

"That's amazing!" I said.

"But wait until you hear this," Joan said. "The Martin people are interviewing in Philadelphia . . . *next week!*"

Another coincidence.

I immediately called Martin and set up an interview for the following Tuesday, just two days after Joan was to return from Denver. The interview went well and resulted in an invitation to fly to Denver for additional interviews the following Friday, which I accepted. In Denver I learned that the Mars Lander was an unmanned vehicle which would soft-land on the surface of Mars and search for signs of life.

That sounded interesting to me, even though I would have to give up my wonderful development lab at GE. Martin's formal offer arrived about ten days later. I accepted it and gave notice of my decision to GE.

When I did so, I learned for the first time that the

81

MOL Project that I'd been working on had been canceled. Another coincidence.

Shortly before my decision to leave GE, I had enrolled in the advanced engineering degree program offered at the Space Division of GE, taught by professors from Brooklyn Polytechnic Institute, and was taking courses for my Master's degree. I was nearly finished with the first course in advanced engineering mathematics when I decided to leave. Not finishing the course would mean no credit. But it had been an excellent refresher course, so I didn't mind. I was now ready for something new.

Maybe Martin Marietta would offer a similar program. They did. Another coincidence.

During my last days at GE I received another surprise. I received an award for a cost-saving idea I had implemented. In addition to the cash bonus (much needed and appreciated at that time), I was allowed to select a gift from one of GE's small appliances. I chose a toaster oven, since ours had been broken just a week earlier. Small though it was, it was still another coincidence.

From the time that Joan suggested the possibility of a move to Denver until the day when we arrived in Denver, less than sixty days had elapsed.

It seemed that, totally outside of ourselves, so many things had been set in motion for our relocation to Denver, and we were just going along for the ride. Even the weather cooperated. This time all four of us drove from Pennsylvania to Denver. Reports of severe snowstorms along our route had prompted me to put our studded snow tires on the car and carry our chains.

But we had good weather for the whole trip. Often

we would hear of blizzards that followed in our wake, just a day after we had passed that way.

We arrived in Denver on October 31, 1969, and checked in to the very Ramada Inn I'd stayed at during my interviews with Martin. That night it snowed. Another coincidence?

9

SKYLAB AND THE HOUND OF HEAVEN

Martin Marietta Aerospace was located in the foothills of the Rocky Mountains, south of Denver, five or six miles from the nearest residential area. Huge red rock outcroppings, reminiscent of Zane Grey's writings, formed a natural picturesque setting for the plant. Dotted amongst the red rock formations one could spot the facades of modern engineering buildings.

If one were to follow the winding highway, past the main plant to the end of the road, he would find the home of the mighty Titan rockets. There he could view the remains of the now dormant test stands of those rockets that testified to the hazards of rocket engine tests of an earlier era. Then he would realize why those tests could not be performed near a city.

Though the tests have long since been completed, the city has not yet crept close to Titan's domain.

We located the plant where I was to work, but finding a home in which we could live was another story.

We couldn't afford a new home, or even a used one for that matter, even though nice ones sold then for less than twenty thousand dollars. So we would rent. But because of the influx of aerospace workers, even homes to rent were difficult to find. For three weeks we searched in vain. We were always either too late, or the house we found was in such poor condition that we wouldn't consider living in it.

Our quest finally came to an end, thanks to our friends Chuck and Shirley Allen, who alerted us to an unadvertised home that a coworker had just vacated. After telephoning the agent, we quickly drove to the location. As we waited, we noted and admired a rather quaint brick house on the corner opposite the one we had come to see. We liked it. After looking at the rental property, which was inadequate for our needs, the realtor asked us if we were interested in the brick house on the corner.

"Yes," we said, "if it's as nice inside as it is out."

"Coincidentally," the realtor said, "it belongs to my father, who is in the hospital recovering from a heart attack." So he showed it to us. In addition to everything else that we liked, the home boasted a large two-car garage, complete with a workbench, built-in air compressor, and a welder.

"We like it," I told the agent. "Can it be rented?"

"Well, I'll ask my father. . . ."

He soon contacted us. "You can have it as is," which included furniture and an old tomcat called Spike. Three days later we occupied the place, moved the owner's furniture to the attic above the garage, and gave the cat away. Finally we could unpack our suitcases. The family loved the home and the huge backyard with its patio and tall flagpole. And I loved the garage, where for the first time since high school I had a place in which to "tinker."

When I reported to work at Martin Marietta, my supervisor informed me that the Viking Project (the Mars Lander Project) had been delayed, so my assignment had changed. Because of my Apollo background, I was assigned to the Skylab Astronaut Medical Experiment Hardware team. Martin Marietta had the contract to provide the medical equipment for Skylab, which would be used by the astronauts to evaluate the effects of living in a zero gravity environment for long periods of time.

I had left the Apollo project because of the death of the astronauts and my desire not to work directly with astronauts again. And now this. I suppressed my apprehension and dug in.

My desk was not in a private office as I had grown used to in my GE lab, but neither was it one of a huge sea of desks like the Apollo days. I was located in a room with about twenty engineers; roughly half of them worked on the Skylab project.

My indoctrination consisted of a few lectures by NASA medical experts, who spoke of the physiology of man in space—the things already known and the things they hoped Skylab would reveal. I cringed a little as they described the experiments the Skylab astronauts were to perform in space. It sounded like they were being used as true guinea pigs, which in a way they were.

My job was to develop the test program for the Skylab medical equipment, to qualify it for flight, then eventually deliver the flight hardware to McDonnell Douglas, where it would be installed in Skylab to be used by the Skylab crews.

The equipment included a blood pressure measuring

system which could automatically take blood pressure readings much as a doctor would do on earth. In operation, an occlusion cuff would be placed around the astronaut's upper arm, then automatically inflated and deflated while a tiny microphone in the cuff picked up the K-sounds and a pressure transducer read the cuff pressure. An electronics box translated the sounds into systolic and diastolic blood pressure and displayed them digitally for the astronaut. The cycle could be repeated automatically or manually, by the push of a button.

Another item of medical equipment we worked on was the "lower body negative pressure device." This consisted of a small chamber, about the size of a fifty-five-gallon drum, into which the astronaut would place his "lower body" (from his waist down), sealing it around the waist. A small negative pressure (vacuum) would be placed on the astronaut's lower body by partially evacuating the chamber. The lowered pressure would cause the astronaut's lower body to "inflate" as it expanded slightly from higher internal pressure, causing blood to rush to his feet, simulating the effect of gravity.

The Skylab experiment would determine if this device would help exercise the parts of the cardiovascular system that deteriorate in space from lack of use. Normally, on earth, gravity pulls the blood toward the feet as we stand, causing tiny, valvelike elements in the veins of our legs to work as the blood is lifted back to the heart. It is these valves that weaken in space when they are not needed for the blood to circulate in zero gravity conditions.

Upon returning to earth, some astronauts found these valves had deteriorated to such a degree that they no longer functioned. When this has happened, gravity pulls blood to the feet, but the valves don't recirculate it and it stays in the feet. As a result, the astronaut passes out. The lower body negative pressure device was designed as a simple substitute for gravity. In space, the Skylab crewmen would use it to exercise their cardiovascular system and so determine if its use would help the men remain healthy.

The most interesting system I had to test was the Sleep Monitoring Experiment. After a few visits to the Houston Medical Research Center, where doctors had been studying the brain waves of sleeping people, I learned that they could identify seven different stages of sleep, in addition to dreaming, by observing a series of brain waves monitored by electrodes on the surface of the scalp.

Our job was to design a system that could detect these levels of sleep electronically, and to design a cap the astronauts could wear as they slept. The cap we finally designed incorporated electrodes made from sponge rubber and filled with a conductive fluid called an electrolyte. On top of the cap we mounted an accelerometer (motion detector), which monitored head movements during sleep.

The sleep experiment was designed to determine how well the astronauts slept in zero gravity. It was believed that sleep could be better than on earth because during sleep in zero gravity the astronaut would not be in contact with a mattress, but would actually "float" in space. During sleep, though, he would be confined to a small sleeping area by a "cage" of lawn-chair type webbing, which would prevent him from drifting too far away from his space.

The doctors explained to me that the quality of sleep

is determined by how much time one spends at each of the various levels of sleep, especially at the deepest level. The sleep monitoring system determined when each level was reached, and recorded it. However, the question that still remained was: How do we know for sure that astronauts sleep better or worse than on earth? To answer that question, we had to take data with the sleep monitoring system while the astronauts slept in their own beds at home.

We installed the system at the bedside of each crew member and connected it to his telephone to relay the data back to NASA. Unfortunately, the spandex sleep caps—complete with electrodes in place—resembled World War I pilot helmets, chin strap and ear openings included. So, when the astronauts donned their "helmets" in preparation for bed, they looked very weird, and the wives complained. We were thus able to gather only minimal sleep data with which to establish our test baseline.

The hardware for the blood pressure measuring system and the sleep monitoring system were subcontracted to a company in Huntsville, Alabama. And since I was responsible for medical equipment qualification and acceptance testing, I spent a lot of time in Huntsville working with the subcontractor, ensuring that the tests met my specifications. In some instances I wrote their procedures for them, which was reminiscent of my Apollo procedure-writing days.

In fact, this new position was more nearly like my Apollo work than my lab supervisor job at GE. But the immeasurable compensation for the difference was the fact that now Joan and the children were happy.

We loved our life in Denver. Although we still had our four-season climate, the winters didn't seem as

SKYLAB AND THE HOUND OF HEAVEN

harsh as those in the East. Somehow the mile-high altitude seemed to make the difference, keeping humidity low, preventing the snows from getting in that wet, slushy stage. And it was so very good to be with our good friends the Allens again.

In the spring of 1970, Martin Marietta Aerospace had their annual employees' picnic at Elitches, Denver's answer to Disneyland. Jack Kurtz, one of the engineers I worked with, invited us to meet him and his family there, to enjoy the day together. Eager to meet people, Joan and I gladly accepted.

Though I had worked with Jack, whom I knew as a thorough, detail-conscious engineer, I was surprised, when I met him and LuAnn, his wife, at the picnic, to learn that he had five children. When Joan and I arrived, and Jack called his children to come and meet us, I was impressed at how well-behaved his large family was. Scott and Sheri, now five and nearly three, were entertained by the Kurtz kids, who showed them a great time on the kiddie rides, while Jack, LuAnn, Joan, and I got to know one another. It was a good day for us all, and all of us got along well; so we invited the Kurtzes to a barbecue in the near future.

The Kurtz family were Christians, we noted, since they always prayed before meals and talked a lot about their church and God's influence in their lives. When Joan, somewhat sheepishly, told them she was Jewish, they were excited. Imagine that: excited! A totally different reaction than that of Christians we'd met before.

On the barbecue day, we had another great time together. At the outset, I offered Jack a beer, which he declined with a polite, "No, thanks." He explained that his father-in-law was an alcoholic, and he had seen the horror such an affliction could bring to a family. He didn't want to give his children the idea that he con-doned the use of alcohol in any form.

I hadn't thought of that concept, and admitted that I admired his integrity—while I drank my beer. During the course of the day I explained my thoughts about God and religion. Jack listened intently. When I fin-ished he said, "I've known other men—especially engi-neers and scientists—who felt the same way."

"*Felt* the same way?" I broke in.

He nodded. "Yes, they felt that way too, until they met Jesus Christ."

That was too much. "C'mon, Jack," I broke in. "He's been dead for almost two thousand years! What do you mean they 'met' Jesus?"

Jack smiled benignly and began, "Stevie (somewhat older than me, Jack loved to call me Stevie, which I al-lowed him to get away with), Jesus is alive today. Right now. He lives in the hearts of all Christians. In my heart as well. And he wants to come into yours." He said all of that looking me straight in the eye.

"Oh, I see," I said. "It's the *teachings* of Jesus that live today. For you surely admit that the man no longer lives . . . is that it?"

"Well, not quite," Jack said. "It's true that his teach-ings live on. But Jesus is a spiritual Person—part of the Trinity of God—and he lives as a spiritual being to-day." Jack always explained things with the utmost pa-tience.

"I thought Jesus was a man, like us," I said. "I haven't heard of this 'spiritual' stuff about Jesus. It sounds like spooks or something." Before Jack could respond, I removed the last hamburger from the grill and called for everyone to "Come and get it."

Just as I bit into my hamburger, Joan suggested that

we have Jack ask a blessing. I quickly swallowed and nodded, "Okay." Jack said the blessing as everyone bowed his head.

Jack prayed a simple but heartfelt prayer, not a trite and "all-purpose" prayer. And as we ate, Jack tried continuing the "Jesus-stuff" talk again, but I always changed the subject. However, before the Kurtzes left for home that day LuAnn asked Joan if she would like to attend church with them.

To my surprise and the Kurtzes' delight, Joan accepted.

"Our church is very close to your home," LuAnn said. "So we'll come by Sunday and pick up you and the children."

Of course I had no interest in going.

During the following week I avoided any contact with Jack at work, thinking it was better to ignore him than to get in an argument with him, because I just didn't understand his religious talk. And at home I questioned Joan several times that week. "Do you know what you're getting into?"

"I think I do," she answered, smiling enigmatically.

"You might get a repeat of the 'Jews killed Jesus' sermon," I warned. But Joan would not be dissuaded. She was more interested in the friendship of the Kurtz family than she was fearful of their pastor's message.

"Besides," she told me, "I'm really curious to see what kind of church they have."

I remembered the name of their church: Calvary Temple. And it *was* just a few blocks from our rented home. I had driven by it many times on the way to work, as well as on the way to visit our friends, the Allens. I knew that the Allens went to church every Sunday, but they were Catholics; so it was a different church. They had never discussed religion with us, which I appreciated. And I attributed their regular attendance to a mere personal habit that began in childhood.

Shortly after we moved into our little brick house, the rental property which had originally drawn us to this corner had been rented by a Chicago couple. We'd become friendly with Carmella and Pete and had learned our way around Denver together. We had even shared a backyard barbecue and an occasional game of bowling. They seemed to be regular "folks" like us, except for their Chicago accent.

The Saturday before Joan and the kids were to go to church with the Kurtzes, Pete and Carmella unexpectedly showed up at our door and asked if they could come in.

"Of course," I said, inviting them in. But the moment I did so, I noted something "different" about them. They came bursting in, their faces aglow with some inner excitement, and for some reason I felt a little apprehensive.

When we got them seated, not knowing quite what to expect, Pete began. "Steve . . . Joan . . . you'll never guess what has happened to us." All the while his face was wreathed with a smile as though he was about to burst into laughter.

Carmella perched on the edge of her seat. "You'll *never* guess," she said, exhibiting even more excitement than her husband. Joan and I glanced at each other and smiled—either with them or because of them, I don't know which.

In his eagerness to tell us what it was that had "happened," Pete's words rushed out, almost on top of each other. "We got saved, Steve. We got saved!"

I felt myself tense up. But there was no stopping him now.

"We went to this church a few blocks down Cherry Creek, and it was fantastic! We talked to one of the pastors there . . . you'd like him, Steve . . . he's very intellectual. And he showed us how we could turn our lives over to Jesus."

In his eagerness to explain, Pete leaned toward us, his face aglow with an unusual light, gesturing with both hands. And though he was evidently trying his best to explain what it was that had happened to him and his wife, to me his words were making very little sense.

"And our whole lives have changed in just a few days," Carmella broke in, ". . . changed in a wonderful way. We've got Jesus in our hearts. And the kids, too!"

Neither Joan nor I said anything while this flow of words came from Pete and Carmella. When they paused, Joan said, "Well, that's nice. We're happy for you." But I could see she was troubled about something. "And this happened at the church called Calvary Temple? Is that the one you're talking about?"

"Yes. That's the one. How did you know? Have you been there?" Pete asked.

"No, but we've heard about it. From a friend that Steve works with. He and his wife invited us to go with them . . . tomorrow." At the moment Joan seemed to be hesitant about the "tomorrow."

"Really? That's great. You're going to love it." Pete and Carmella were both excited now. "And that's the reason we came over today—to invite you to come with us. It's a super church!"

"I'm going to go with Scott and Sheri," Joan volunteered.

95

Pete looked at me for confirmation. I said nothing. He was incredulous. "You mean you aren't going? I know you don't think much of religion and all that, but you ought to go and hear this intellectual preacher. His name is Pastor Jim Spillman. I know you'd enjoy him, Steve. And Pastor Blair, too. He's the head pastor. He's really a great preacher, too. They've got several pastors there. It's a big church."

"Well, church is just not for me," I said rather lamely.

"Don't you want to go and see what your own wife and kids are getting into?" Carmella asked.

I hadn't thought of that angle. I knew that if Joan were to go and then come home in tears again, I would be curious about what had happened. Pete and Carmella sounded so sincere. And until now I'd thought they were levelheaded. But it was very evident that something *had* happened. Something had changed them. And this Spillman: an intellectual pastor? That seemed like a contradiction of terms. *Maybe I should go and check this thing out,* I thought. *Just once.*

"Well," I said slowly, "since it means so much to you, I'll go . . . but just this once." Joan looked at me in wonderment, but I ignored her glance.

"That's great, Steve!" Pete said. "Maybe we'll see you there. They have an early service, then a Sunday school, then a later service. That one's televised. Which one are you going to?"

I was stunned. Surely there couldn't be *that* many people going to church! I shrugged, not knowing how to answer. Joan spoke up. "The Kurtzes are picking us up about 9:30."

Pete brightened. "Oh, then you must be going to

Sunday school first. Good. Be sure to go to Pastor Spillman's class."

Pete grabbed my hand and shook it like a long-lost friend, and Carmella gave Joan a hug. "We'll see you there." The last thing I saw as they went out the door was their Cheshire cat grins.

As soon as the door closed, Joan said, "I'm glad you decided to go with us." She looked at me closely. "I hope you're serious and won't back out in the morning. . . ."

I know she expected some sort of rebuttal from me, but I held my peace. Because I'd already thought of the best reason in the world why I *should* go: Now I could get some firsthand ammunition about how these stupid churches and religions really work. I would gather it all and use it as evidence for my reasons never to go again.

I thought all that, but I merely said to Joan, "I'll go. You'll see . . ."

10

AN ATHEIST
AND A JEW
IN CHURCH

Sunday morning dawned bright and clear. And as the bright Denver sunlight filtered through the curtains of our bedroom, I lay there thinking: This is the day our family is to attend church. I also thought of my headache. But I knew if I mentioned that to Joan, she would accuse me of inventing it as an excuse to avoid going to church with her and the kids.

Instead of discussing my throbbing head, I acted as brightly as possible under the circumstances. "I'll bet Jack and LuAnn will be surprised when they see me going with you," I said.

Joan hardly paused in her preparations. "They already know," she said with a smile. "I called LuAnn last night."

"You did?"

"Yes. I told her about Pete and Carmella's visit."

"What did she say?"

"She was pleased that you'd decided to go. She even

got excited about Pete and Carmella, even though she said she didn't know them."

I groaned inwardly. It would be difficult to avoid Jack at the office now. He'd probably want us to go back to his church again. And even the neighbors would be pestering us, I thought. But then maybe we could move to another house when our year's agreement was up.

All of this and more ran through my head as we ate breakfast and got ourselves ready to go. When we arrived at Calvary Temple, to my utter amazement the parking lot was jammed. But that seemed not to faze Jack, and we followed him as he drove to an auxiliary lot across the street.

Because Jack was a member of the choir, he had to dash off. But LuAnn directed us to Pastor Jim Spillman's Sunday school class, explaining, "This is only one of the adult classes that are available."

Hardly knowing what to expect, we entered an auditoriumlike room and sat down among a couple of hundred other people. I saw Pete and Carmella across the room. They started to join us, but a man began leading the group in singing. After everybody (except us) sang several songs from memory (Joan and I had never heard any of them before), a nice-looking gentleman stood up to speak.

"Is that Spillman?" I whispered to LuAnn.

She shook her head in the negative.

"Pastor Spillman is speaking at another church this morning," the teacher said, "so I'm substituting for him."

Then the substitute teacher launched into a "lesson" that made hardly any sense to me. He used a lot of terms that were so strange to me he could have been using a foreign language. He referred often to the "Holy Ghost" and what "he" could do in one's life. I wondered if the others were making any more of the teacher's jargonese than I was.

I glanced around the room. And to my surprise, some people were avidly listening to every word the teacher spoke. Many were taking copious notes. Others were nodding in agreement with the speaker's subject matter. My eye caught Pete's, and he smiled at me. He said something to his wife, and she smiled at me from across the room. They both seemed to be thoroughly enjoying the entire experience.

I wondered if I was the only person present who had no idea what this fellow was talking about.

As he was winding down, somebody passed a basket of money past us. I reached for my wallet to contribute, but LuAnn shook her head. "Let's keep the basket moving," she said. "There'll be another offering in the next service."

The next service? I thought, sighing to myself. I hadn't known about that.

But when the class ended, LuAnn led Joan and me upstairs to what she called "the main sanctuary." I was stunned by the size of the place, and the vast number of people beginning to assemble! Mentally I calculated that there had to be at least two thousand in this main sanctuary. And I'd thought the two hundred in our class had been a lot. *Could there be this many people in Denver who needed a crutch?* I wondered.

LuAnn undoubtedly saw the amazement written on my face. She smiled and informed us that "This is the second service of the morning." The *second* service! I was dumbfounded. For what possible reason did all of these people come to church? Entertainment perhaps?

Or social satisfaction? Or possibly it was just the continuation of a childhood habit. At any rate, it was undeniable that they were here in droves, with Joan and myself among them.

Seated in that huge sanctuary, I felt uncomfortably ill at ease and out of place. I supposed that merely being in church with all of these others implied some degree of accord with religion, a thought that repelled me. I was certainly not about to stoop to any agreement in such matters with all of these strange-thinking people.

Just then the bright lights turned on and I saw the television cameras being moved into place. A strange nervousness came over me as I realized that someone I knew might see me in this church audience and get the wrong idea.

I was aware of LuAnn speaking. "I want you to meet Steve and Joan Carman . . . it's their first time," she was saying to a couple behind us.

The nicely-dressed man was friendly. "First-timers?" he said. "Praise the Lord!" I smiled back, thinking, *Yeah, first-timers and last-timers too.*

The Kurtz kids joined us, filling the padded bench. I squeezed Joan's hand. "How're you doing?"

She whispered back, "I'm okay. How're you doing?"

"I'm ready to go home."

She frowned slightly, but squeezed my hand in return.

Just then the red-robed choir paraded in, filling several rows of the benchlike seats on the stage. I spotted Jack among them and nodded to him. Then six men dressed in black suits came on stage from the wings and sat down on the seats in front of the choir. One of those six men stood up and led the choir in an opening song. *Not bad for a choir,* I thought.

I turned to LuAnn. "Does Jack sing baritone?"

She whispered back. "No, he's a tenor."

The choir sat down, and another man came to the podium and pleasantly welcomed all the people. He asked all newcomers to stand up (now I was really embarrassed!) and to fill out a card, giving our names, addresses, and a bunch of other very personal data. I shoved the card in my pocket. No sense having someone else stalking us as prospects for this church.

After some congregational singing from a songbook which they called a "hymnal" (located in a rack on the back of the seat in front of us), the choir stood up and sang a couple more songs. Then another man—the one who'd taught our Sunday school class—stood and took the "offering." I was ready this time, and as the offering basket was passed, I put some money on top of the stack.

Finally the senior pastor, Pastor Charles Blair, came to the podium. He announced that the topic for his sermon was, "Is There *Really* a Devil?"

I could hardly believe what I was hearing! How could anyone in this space age believe in even the possibility of there being a devil? And even if he believed in such an archaic thought, why would he take time to seriously discuss the matter?

I nudged Joan with my elbow. When she looked at me, I rolled my eyes heavenward as if to say, "Oh, brother! You've got to be kidding!" I chuckled inside, thinking I was about to be provided with a perfect example of why none of us should ever attend church again. Despite my superior attitude and my mental resistance, that sermon was to leave a lasting impact upon my mind.

Pastor Blair spoke plainly, using English words I could understand, avoiding the "Christianese" that had been so prevalent in the Sunday school class. He skillfully explained the evidence for the existence of the spirit world, in which there was an ongoing battle between good and evil, between God and Satan. I was impressed with his intelligent, logical presentation of facts and the manner in which he answered my questions and overcame my objections almost as fast as they arose in my mind.

In fact, it seemed that he had prepared his talk just for me!

Not that I necessarily agreed with everything the pastor said, which I didn't. But as Charles Blair spoke forcefully from his own experience with this spirit world, I sensed his sincere, honest conviction. And I had no reason to doubt that he truly believed what he was saying.

He declared that all children, as descendants of the original sinners, are born with the same sinful nature and that they don't have to be taught to be naughty or bad, because that's their natural inclination. Instead, they must be taught to be good. I found this line of reasoning offensive, for I had always believed that man was fundamentally good. Nevertheless, I was forced to concede the point with Pastor Blair, because my own experience with my two children coincided with his claim. I had had to teach them to be good.

But as Pastor Blair spoke that first day, he did introduce me to a dimension of man that I had never heard before. For the first time in my life, a spark of curiosity in this "religious stuff" was awakened in me. Also, for the first time I could begin to understand how some people might actually believe in this spiritual dimension. But I was still unconvinced. It was not for me.

On the way home Joan and I talked about our experience. "How did you like it?" I asked.

She shrugged. "It was okay. I liked the people we met. But the preaching about Jesus was disturbing." Joan's Jewish heritage and environment had rooted in her an aversion to the name Jesus, and had taught her to be guarded around Christians, because they were out to "convert" the Jews.

Scott and Sheri, with lollipops in their mouths, nodded their affirmative evaluation of the church.

"It was nice of Jack and LuAnn to invite us," I said, "but I have no desire to return." Joan agreed. Scott was about to complain about my nonreturn decision, but quickly changed his tune when I turned and scowled at him.

While Joan was preparing dinner, I thought about Pastor Blair's sermon. He had repeatedly cited verses from the Bible to validate the thesis of his message, claiming the Bible to be "the infallible Word of God—true from cover to cover."

While I had never been overtly antagonistic toward church folk, I had always put down those who quoted from the Bible, claiming it to be "God's Word." My position was that the words in the Bible were written by men, not God. Therefore, it was just another book produced by religious fanatics in an age before science had eliminated many superstitions and fears that had caused them to "invent" God. God was merely man's creation to explain what science could not explain. Ultimately, science would discover an explanation for everything and God would no longer be necessary.

Yet, I had to admit I had arrived at such a philosophy without ever having read the Bible. And I had never experienced any desire to read it. But now, after having heard this man so strongly advocate the infallibility of the Bible, I realized that I could not talk intelligently to these Christians about either the nature or contents of the Bible if I had never read it. So I decided that I would read the Bible.

That presented me with a dilemma. How was I to get hold of one? I casually approached Joan. "Do you know where we can get a Bible?" I asked her.

She looked at me quizzically. "Well . . . the Kurtzes would probably loan us one if we asked them."

"Don't you have a Jewish Bible?" I asked. I didn't want to borrow a Bible from Jack. I didn't want him to think that our visit to his church had stimulated me to begin reading the Bible.

After thinking a moment, Joan said, "I remember receiving a small Old Testament at my *Bat Mitzvah* when I was thirteen. But I don't know where it is . . . unless it's stored with my old university books."

In our small house we had limited bookshelf space, so we had stored many boxes of books in a crawl space under our house. Some of those books were from our university classes, but most of them were books I'd inherited from my parents (both had been avid readers).

I located a flashlight and crawled into the storage area through the access door in the floor of Scott's closet. Scott came with me to hold the flashlight. To my dismay, I saw that two boxes had become soaked with ground water and the books in them were ruined. I finally found a box of Joan's books and laboriously moved it up through the crawl space into Scott's room. Joan and I sorted through her old books one at a time. The Old Testament was not among them.

Back in the hole I went, and began going through the many boxes of my parents' books, something I'd wanted to do, but had never found time. I opened box after box. The books were mostly fiction, primarily mysteries. I was about to give up when I noted something different about the next box.

The first thing I saw when I opened it were two picture albums. Immediately below that was a really ornate antique album filled with old tintypes of people I had never known. I leafed through the albums, then put them aside and dug deeper. I found Dad's collection of earned medals and awards, most of them from his high school athletics.

The sight of these awards awakened memories. Down in the musty crawl space I made myself as comfortable as possible and shared some of Dad's stories with Scott. One of them had to do with his first high school track meet. Though not a member of the track team, the coach had allowed Dad to go along to help out with the equipment. Midway in the meet a crisis occurred when the school's only shot-putter twisted his ankle and was unable to participate. When Dad told me the story, he had paused at this point.

"What happened?" I had asked him.

He grinned that old familiar grin. "I asked the coach if I could substitute. . . ."

"And he let you?" I asked breathlessly.

"He had no substitute, so he really had no choice."

"Then what?" I probed.

"Well, Steve, I not only participated in the event, but I set a new record for Susanville High School, and won this medal."

Now, as I told the story to my son, I guessed which

of these moldy medals had been awarded to his grandfather for that long ago victory.

The story over, I dug even deeper into this box. And then, in the uncertain light of Scott's wavering flashlight, I came across a heavy, black, leather-bound volume. Unbidden, my heart pounded as I pried it out of its resting place, turned it on edge, and read the gold printing on the spine. Even in the semidarkness of the crawl space I could make out the title.

It read: *Holy Bible*.

11

THE OLD
STORY
BECOMES
NEW

With dusty fingers, I lifted and held the old book. Thinking it must be Joan's Bible, and wondering how it had gotten mixed with my Dad's things, I opened it. I was surprised to see that it was not the Old Testament, but a whole Bible. And it looked brand new. The fine leather cover was unscratched and unworn. The edges of the pages were still a like-new shiny gold. And when I opened it, the pages clung together as though they had never been parted from the day they left the bindery.

Clearly this was not the Bible Joan had described to me as hers. Then whose was it? And where had it come from? There was a small Christmas sticker pasted inside the front cover, but that gave me no clue to the Bible's ownership.

I climbed from the crawl space, sat down, and leafed through the first few pages until I found the inscription, which I read with astonishment.

"Joan," I called. "See what I found."

My wife joined me immediately. I handed the Bible to her. "Look," I said. "I found a Bible. But it wasn't yours . . . and you'll never guess where it came from."

I opened the inscription page and read to her:

Presented to: Donald L. Carman
From: Grandma Atha Carman
Occasion: Christmas 1936
Date: December 25, 1936

"Donald L. Carman . . . that was your father? It was his Bible!" She looked at me in astonishment. "But . . . but didn't you tell me that your family never had a Bible?"

I nodded. "That's what I thought. I never knew Dad had this. Maybe he even forgot that he had it."

I remembered that on one of the few occasions when religion had been discussed in our home, Dad had told me about his stepmother's rigid Catholic beliefs and how she insisted that he attend mass regularly.

"But I never got anything out of it," Dad told me that day. "Religion's superfluous," he said. "It's for the people who need a crutch. But it's not for me. And not for my family."

And now, holding my dead father's old but unused Bible in my hands, I was very moved. "That's what Dad once told me," I said to my wife. "And after today's experience in church I can see his point. Can't you?"

"Maybe," Joan conceded. "But I do like LuAnn and Jack. And I'd like to be friends with them. You know, we've never made any real close friends. . . ."

I knew she was right. Even though we did have and

had always had friends, we seemed always to have avoided close relationships with them.

"Besides," she went on, "don't you work with Jack in the same office?"

"We were in the same office until recently," I said. "He's been moved to another location. But I do usually see him around." I didn't tell Joan that I had been avoiding Jack because of his "Jesus talk."

I changed the subject then, talking about Atha, my Dad's grandmother. Joan saw through that and answered me briefly, then went right to the point. "Now that you've found a Bible, are you going to read it?"

I grinned. "Well, at least I'll look at the pictures," I said as I flipped through the nonillustrated Bible. Despite my attempt at flippancy, I was aware of an unaccustomed excitement over the discovery of my dad's Bible. I thought it to be quite a coincidence that I should discover this family heirloom just when I had determined to read the "Good Book" for myself—even if my motive was to expose its flaws.

But how should I read this Bible?

My technical training had caused me to become a very slow, methodical reader, always beginning with page one and plowing through every single word, paragraph, and page until I reached the end. Since my reading consisted mostly of technical matter, I honestly believed this was the only logical way to read. There wasn't any way you could spot-read a mathematics textbook. It wouldn't be reasonable to skip a few pages or paragraphs in such a book, then expect to understand every concept. And why should I expect reading the Bible to be any different?

So, consistent with my usual practice, I opened the

Bible to page one, line one, and began reading.

"In the beginning God created the heavens and the earth."

I had read scarcely more than a few words when I was at odds with Pastor Blair's claim that the Bible was "truth from start to finish." My disagreement with him began with the Genesis account of creation. Pastor Blair claimed that all this was the truth. But even I could see that the "seven-day creation story" and the Adam and Eve account were obviously ancient fables that had been written in some unenlightened age before Darwin had discovered the "real truth" of evolution.

Doubtless all this interesting story had been made up and handed down from generation to generation for thousands of years in an attempt to answer the question, "Where did we come from?"

I read through several chapters of Genesis, not always comprehending the King James Version's old English. I thought the Flood story was another interesting myth. I finally lost interest when I came to Chapter 10's list of generations. Then, after thumbing randomly through several other parts of this unfamiliar Book, I put it down and wandered into the kitchen, where Joan was preparing one of her culinary specialties.

She looked up and smiled at me. "What have you been doing?"

"Well, I just read a few pages of Dad's Bible . . . stories about Adam and Eve, and Noah and the Flood. Stuff like that."

"Like it?" Her question threw me. I hadn't expected to like the Bible. It was an old religious book that was to be read as much for curiosity as enjoyment.

I hedged. "Well, I read enough of it to know that I can't agree with Pastor Blair."

"What do you mean?" Joan asked.

"He said the Bible was all true. But those stories about the origin of things that I read are just ancient myths as far as I'm concerned."

She looked at me curiously. "Did you read any of the New Testament?"

I was surprised at her question. "The New Testament? I didn't think you would read any of that stuff about Jesus."

She shrugged. "I'm not sure I would. I just wondered if you had read any of it yourself."

"No, not really," I said. "I just sort of thumbed through it. I'll read it some other time." I sniffed. "What's cooking?"

The following week when I saw Jack Kurtz at the office he said, "Stevie, I was disappointed that you didn't get to meet Pastor Spillman Sunday."

I shrugged. "Well, that's all right."

Jack wasn't finished. He went on, "But Wednesday night I told Pastor Spillman you wanted to meet him, and he said he was looking forward to meeting you and your family."

When I didn't respond, Jack said, "Do you want us to meet you and go to church with you this Sunday?"

"Well, I guess we could just meet you there, Jack," I said. "That is . . . if we decide to go again." I was eager to get back to my work and not be bothered by all this religious stuff. It didn't seem to fit into my world of space project engineering.

But Jack wasn't to be so easily put off. "Oh, I see . . . another commitment?"

"Not really. It's just that Joan is Jewish. And she finds all that talk about Jesus a little offensive. And I'm not sure that I go along with the preacher's sermons either."

"Well, if you don't make it Sunday, maybe you can meet Pastor Spillman some other time. Like Wednesday night."

"Wednesday night?" I said. "You go to church twice a week?" I was beginning to think that Jack was a *real* fanatic.

He smiled. "Stevie, in a church the size of Calvary Temple, some weeks there's something going on every night. But during a regular week we've got services both Sunday morning and night. Besides that, there's choir practice, Sunday school meetings, and all kinds of special activities."

Despite myself, I was amazed at Jack. He really *was* a fanatic to be so heavily involved in church things. Yet he was such a sharp engineer. It didn't add up. How could anyone so obviously intelligent as Jack believe all those Bible stories—those myths—and waste all that time in church?

I just shook my head. "Look, Jack," I said, "I've got to get back to work. I'll discuss all this with Joan, and if we decide to go to church I'll give you a call."

"Okay, Stevie," Jack answered sincerely. "I hope you can make it."

I was glad to get back to my work. Talking about church with Jack made me nervous. Someone might get the wrong idea, and then my credibility would be shot. And I certainly had no intention of ever going near that church or any other church again.

During the week Joan picked up Dad's Bible and read several chapters. For different reasons, she found it as frustrating as I had. My frustration had arisen from sheer unbelief, hers because she *wanted to understand,* but couldn't. She also talked with her newfound friend LuAnn, who had invited her to attend church again on the following Sunday. Joan told me about the invitation.

"Naturally you refused," I said.

"No, I told LuAnn I would go with her."

Instantly angry, I said, "Why didn't you ask me first?"

"Because I wasn't sure you'd want to go again. Anyway, you can stay home if you want to. But the kids and I had a good time, so I think we should give them some religious education. . . ."

I was fuming, but she wasn't finished.

"Besides, I would like to meet this Pastor Spillman they all talk about. Wouldn't you?"

I didn't answer directly. "What about all this Jesus stuff? I thought it irritated you."

"It does. But while it's not for me, I *do* like the people we met. There's something special about them. They're all so nice and friendly . . . the kind of friends I'd like to have."

"We can meet lots of people without going to church," I burst out. "Nice people. People who aren't religious fanatics. Do you realize that Jack and LuAnn go to church three or four times *each week?*"

Joan smiled. "It doesn't matter, Steve. If you were as involved in something as they are in church, you'd spend a lot of time studying it too. In fact, you do. When you're deeply involved in a project, that's about all you think about . . . all you talk about, isn't it?"

Seeing all this talk was making me angry, Joan paused and hugged me before she continued.

"Steve, you know how much I like people. And when I meet folk I enjoy being with and have a lot of fun with, I want them to be our friends."

She paused and I continued to fume, though I was cooling down a little. "And, Steve, I don't want to make you mad over this church thing . . . I *know* how you feel about religion." She spoke warmly, but firmly. "But whether you want to go or not, I would like to take the kids again, at least one more time. Okay?"

I had never been able to resist Joan's straightforward logic. I shrugged. "Sure. If you want to go, then go. I can use the time to get some reading done. But if you don't mind, I'm going to retire from my churchgoing days . . . forever."

12

MY DILEMMA

What was I to do? Joan had made her concerned-about-the-kids speech, which I'd countered with my head-of-the-house position. It could have ended in an impasse, but it didn't. Joan is much too wise a wife to allow that to happen. She just sweetly moved through the week with the assumption that she and the kids would be going to church, with or without me. No big battle or scene. Just fact.

What *was* I to do?

I was a space scientist. And as such, I felt a certain responsibility to my profession, and to my peers. Exactly what that position was or should have been regarding religion, I would have been hard pressed to state or defend. However . . .

As a space scientist I had watched with great interest (and not a little nervousness) the historic moon landing of Apollo 11 in July 1969. Clearly the redesigned spacecraft had successfully corrected the defects that

117

had been so evident after the tragic fire in Apollo 1. I was as thrilled as a kid when I saw Neil Armstrong first set foot on that mysterious lunar surface and heard, along with millions of others, his dynamic statement, "One small step for man, one giant leap for mankind."

There on the moon the astronauts found no "moon germs." But they did learn that the moon and the earth were composed of the same basic minerals. Then, in November of the same year, Apollo 12 skillfully repeated that earlier lunar moon landing. It went off without a single hitch. Practically "routine."

However, a few months later, in April of the following year, near disaster struck Apollo 13—moonward bound, 205,000 miles from the earth. One of the main oxygen tanks exploded, causing all sorts of problems. As an involved scientist who had known other astronauts who had placed their lives in jeopardy, I was deeply concerned. But after a suspenseful four days, Apollo 13 made it home safely, thanks to some quick thinking by the crew and engineers back home.

As each of these space missions occupied my mind, I found myself persistently faced with the question of whether or not I, as a scientist, had the responsibility of refuting God and standing up for science. Or should I just keep my mouth shut and let these church people go ignorantly on their way? It was a question I was to struggle with for months.

At any rate, as the first anniversary of the Apollo 11 lunar landing approached, Steve Carman, confirmed atheist, and Joan Carman, his Jewish wife, were taking their children to a Christian church *every Sunday*!

And as I sat in church each Sunday, I was continuously amazed at all these twentieth-century people who could still believe in all the ancient myths and fables I was hearing preached as truth. And in some not-as-yet-understood way (at least for me), the hearing of such "myths and fables" seemed to supply these church people with a certain missing ingredient, an ingredient I arrogantly assured myself I didn't lack. Yet, when I allowed myself to honestly admit it, I knew there was something missing in my life. I had a void, an emptiness I couldn't fill. For six years I had assumed that the loss of my parents had caused that void.

But as I observed the calm assurance evidenced by the Christians around me, I was forced to analyze my own lack of that kind of peaceful confidence. I couldn't understand how their faith could enable them to face all their problems with such serenity and stability. Even more mysterious to me was their calm acceptance that the outcome of these problems was part of a master plan that was working for their common good.

Yes, the void was there in my life. I had to face that fact. And these Christians seemed to have found something to fill whatever void they might have had.

So perhaps it was the desire to fill that emptiness with something meaningful that kept me going to Calvary Temple. I'm sure my regular attendance was piqued by my curiosity to meet Pastor Jim Spillman (the "intellectual pastor"). Or, it might have been the gentle and loving encouragement of the Kurtz family that did it, coupled with my very human desire to be with my family on Sundays. It might have been a combination of all these reasons.

Nevertheless, despite my resistance, I found myself thinking about God much of the time—in fact, more so than in all of my previous life. I still honestly believed that God was an invention of man. But now I was willing to concede that this "invention" might actually have some merit. After all, there seemed to be a lot of people who apparently derived great pleasure from pretending there was a Supreme Being who cared for them.

My dissonance was compounded when I asked myself how any honest scientist could even superficially give mental assent to this "invented" God and still maintain a credible attitude toward his technical work. This, I was forced to admit, would be next to impossible, because the very foundation of the scientific method was based on an unbiased, rational analysis of any problem which would proceed from the observed "evidence" to logical conclusions. That was the essence of my problem with God. Who could demonstrate God? Who could actually prove his existence?

Certainly, then, to believe in God would require the setting aside of logic and accepting an undemonstrated idea in the total absence of evidence. Could I, as a scientist, do that?

Perhaps this wonder man, Pastor Jim Spillman, would be able to shed some light on the subject. My image of an "intellectual pastor," as Spillman had been portrayed to me, was one of a middle-aged, balding, slightly stooped, bespectacled professor-type, with a huge Bible tucked under his arm, who went around expounding Scripture with every breath.

I was surprised to find the real-life Jim Spillman to be the good-looking, six foot five, quick-witted redhead that he was. When I saw this imposing hulk of a man, I sat up and took notice. But when Pastor Spillman opened his mouth to speak, I sat up even straighter. This man evidently had something to say that was worth listening to.

Pastor Jim's talks (or "messages," as they were called in the Christian jargon I was learning to interpret) weren't at all the dull, unimaginative monologues I expected. They were stimulating, dynamic, and most of all, practical. His everyday applications of Scripture always provided me with the proverbial food for thought.

One of Spillman's favorite methods of exploring a subject or Bible passage was his "scientific" approach to words. Dissatisfied with a mere "Webster's definition" of a word, Jim would go to the original language, translate it for us, give us the word's etymology, and trace its progressive development from its origin to the present time and usage.

Despite my admitted prejudice, I was impressed by his thoroughness. And by his humor, which I enjoyed immensely. I soon found myself eagerly looking forward to Pastor Jim's Sunday morning teachings.

Pastor Blair was equally stimulating, and his messages always seemed to focus on my personal situation. He frequently invited guest speakers to preach, which provided the congregation (including Joan and me) with exposure to a wide variety of Scripture interpretations and applications. I will never forget the inimitable Charles "Tremendous" Jones, so called because of his frequent use of his favorite adjective. I was deeply impressed by the scholarly look and preaching of Dr. J. Sidlow Baxter. Both Joan and I loved his heavy British accent. Dr. Baxter presented an amazing exposition of the books of the Bible, explaining that "God must have had a hand in the creation of such a Book."

But for a steady diet, Pastor Blair's preaching was hard to beat. His presentations were current, but he always focused on the ancient Scriptures by applying them to modern problems. And you could always count on Pastor Blair giving an "invitation" at the close of each service for people to "come forward" to "accept Jesus."

Personally, I wasn't about to "accept" anything I didn't clearly understand, and there were many such things. So I steadfastly resisted "going forward" with the others. And Joan's resistance to the "invitation" was a very Jewish thing. She longed to have "all of God," but she wanted nothing to do with the Christian's Jesus. So she never went forward to the altar either. Despite this passive resistance, we continued to go to the church and were there about every time the doors were open, because we enjoyed the excellent teaching concerning a good, moral life-style.

After about three months of this, it became evident to both of us that we were arriving at some sort of a crisis, and that we could not continue attending Calvary Temple without making some sort of a decision.

On the one hand, we longed to possess the joy that emanated from those who "believed," a joy they attributed to their faith in Jesus Christ. But neither Joan nor I could accept this weekly invitation and become one of the "believers." As a Jewess, Joan couldn't believe that Jesus was the "Son of God." And as an atheist, I couldn't even believe there was a God.

All these months we found ourselves experiencing a sort of dynamic tension. And I began compiling a mental list of issues which the church's teachers and preachers had not addressed to my personal satisfaction. I didn't really expect these issues to be addressed from the pulpit, for many of them required a technical background to understand adequately or to address the very real inner conflicts I wrestled with.

To Joan, I referred to my list as the "pastor stumpers," a term she was in agreement with because she too had questions. Though hers were different than mine, hers were no less valid, having to do with the Messiahship of Jesus, and why it was so necessary to accept him instead of just accepting God.

Jack had provided me with a few articles and books written by scientists who were Christians. I had read a few of their "defenses" of the faith, but none of them completely satisfied my inquiring mind.

I felt that if God were real, he would have provided us with some unambiguous, concrete evidence. After all, I reasoned, if he was really the all-powerful Creator we were being led to believe, surely he could provide a rational thinker with enough tangible facts to conclude that there was a God. While there was an abundance of "secondary evidence," such as the effect God had on people's lives, there was very little, if any, "primary evidence" of his existence.

This "primary evidence" I defined as instances where people had actually seen God, or a "measurable" change in a person's life, or the miraculous healing of a body. Yet, as far as I was concerned, even such healings could not always be considered as bona fide evidence of God's intervention, since I believed that healings could be the result of a natural process in the body which enabled the body to heal itself.

Yet, wherever I turned, the answer I sought always seemed to hinge on some degree of a blind acceptance of something I could not see, touch, taste, hear, or measure. And this blind acceptance was necessary, it seemed, which for me would only be the confirmation of the preconceived notion that God was actually a man-made idea. It was a vicious circle. Time after time

I reasoned myself into a blind alley from which I could not extricate myself.

I became obsessed with this lack of clear evidence. And it became the subject of almost every conversation, both at home and at work. Jack patiently listened to my questions, and we spent many evenings discussing them.

Sometimes we'd begin our discussion immediately after work as we walked to our cars. And often we'd end up spending an hour or two in the parking lot. Very often our wives wondered where their husbands were. Frequently both Jack and I came home to an overcooked dinner (or, worse yet, cold).

Our conversations were never dull, though they were sometimes repetitive. I was insistent upon verifiable truth. Jack was persistent, patient, and—mostly—logical.

"I hear what you're saying, Jack," I said over and over again. "But try to hear what I'm saying. Okay?"

"Okay, I'll try."

"Pastor Blair teaches us that the Bible is God's Word. That it's the truth. From cover to cover. Right?"

"That's right, Stevie. And it is!"

"And you actually believe that?" I pressed.

"Yes, Stevie," he'd always answer. "Yes, I believe it. Unequivocally. But I more than believe it. I *know* it."

"All right, Jack," I said. "Let's take it from the top. Starting with the first chapter of Genesis, verse 1. Do you believe that God created the universe? Do you *honestly* believe that?"

He nodded. "Yes, I do. And I can understand your confusion. You see, Stevie, secular schools and universities don't give the student the biblical perspective on the origin of the universe, or on the origin of life in the universe. Right?"

"Of course," I agreed, thinking that such teaching would have been sufficient grounds for a professor's dismissal at Berkeley. "But they teach what they believe is the true origin of the universe. Like the Big Bang and all that."

"You're right, Stevie," Jack continued, "but those schools teach how everything evolved from that *accidental* beginning. Everything. The earth, plants, animals, man, everything. But the probability of such events happening accidentally is so small, so infinitesimal, that evolution would be considered impossible."

I set my briefcase down and shifted to a better position.

Jack took a deep breath and went on. "And that probability is so low that if it were applied to any other event, it would be an impossibility. Such as the probability that a Swiss watch would assemble itself from a box of raw materials. And yet men insist upon the evolutionary explanation of the universe to give them a reason to ignore God."

I broke in. "Wait a minute, Jack. Do you really think that men use evolution as an excuse to ignore God?"

"Well, that may not have been Darwin's motivation. But many men have certainly tried to make names for themselves by 'discovering' the so-called missing link, claiming they had proof that man evolved from the apes. But their discoveries are usually skeletal remnants that they claim are those of an ancient ape-man. And what the professors don't tell you is that closer examination proves many of these 'discoveries' to be hoaxes."

"I know that, Jack," I said. "Those men were just phony scientists trying to promote themselves. But that doesn't necessarily mean they were ignoring God. Or that evolution is not still going on."

"Stevie, let's assume for the moment that evolutionists are right, and that everything has evolved to where we are today. That would mean that as one species evolved into another—grass into wheat, monkey into man, or whatever—that there should be a lot of these transitional life forms being found in the fossils the archaeologists find. Isn't that right?"

I shrugged. "Seems logical. But I'm not an archaeologist."

Jack chuckled. "Neither am I. But the fact is, Stevie, that there are *many* 'missing links' in the evolutionary chain—not just the half-man, half-ape link. There are so many of these missing links that one must question the validity of the evolutionary theory. . . ."

He paused momentarily. "In fact, Stevie, the truth of the matter is that the fossil records provide a better support for a creationist theory of the sudden appearance of species than the evolutionary theory."

"I find that hard to believe, Jack."

"Check it out for yourself."

"Okay, I'll do that. But, Jack, if that's true, why wouldn't my professors have pointed this out, at least as an alternative theory?"

Jack shook his head. "Because a man believes what he wants to believe. And sometimes a man would rather believe a lie than to accept the alternative—that there is an almighty Creator."

Day after day, week after week our dialogue continued. At the office. In the parking lot. At church. In our backyards. We covered a lot of territory, and I revealed to Jack a number of my pastor stumpers—Noah's ark and the Flood, or miracles that defied logic, such as raising a man from the dead. Still, I failed to see that "accepting Jesus" was a logical solution, or conclusion, to any of this.

Jack and I often worked together on the Skylab experimental hardware, and I respected him for his technical abilities. There was no doubt in my mind that Jack was transparently sincere, that he loved the Lord deeply, and that he practiced what he preached. Joan and I were often in their home, and they in ours. So I saw him under all sorts of conditions with his coworkers and his wife and family, and I was always impressed by his consistent, loving kindness to all he met.

And when Jack talked about the "sacrifice" that Christ made on the cross, tears would inevitably well up in his eyes and he would get all choked up. It was as though he *believed* that Christ had died for Jack Kurtz personally.

I could not doubt Jack's sincerity, nor the evidence of his life. But he was Jack and I was Steve. We were two different people. Maybe Jack needed some sort of a crutch that I didn't need.

And maybe it was the other way around. Maybe I needed something that Jack already had.

Maybe, just maybe, Jack was right.

13

JOAN'S WATERLOO

By this time, getting ready for church was a routine. We'd get dressed, then I'd grab Dad's Bible and a box of tissues. The Bible was for me—to check up on what the preachers were reading and saying. The tissues were for Joan—she cried through most services and was continually wiping away her tears. She was very tender and would empathetically weep when anyone shared how God had moved in his life.

At times, Joan would cry at the slightest thing spoken from the pulpit. Once an announcement was made concerning someone leaving their lights on in the parking lot. I turned to Joan, and to my astonishment she was weeping. Without a word I handed her another tissue.

During one Wednesday evening service, just after Joan had depleted a major portion of our tissue supply, an elderly lady patted Joan on the shoulder and said, "It's just the Holy Spirit, dear." Joan and I looked at her, then at each other. Simultaneously we shrugged our shoulders in total lack of comprehension.

Finally, Joan and I agreed we could no longer continue to attend church in a state of confusion. Something had to be done about it. But what? Joan didn't want to have anything to do with Jesus; she just wanted more of God. And at the same time she longed to possess the quality of life she saw in those Christians. For me, I wasn't about to make a move until I could logically rationalize this new spiritual dimension of man we'd been exposed to.

But we were in a quandary. We seemingly had no options. We weren't invited to "Come, get to know God better." Or, "Come, and let's reason all of this through." The only "invitation" that was given was to "come forward and give your life to Jesus." Joan's orientation was, "Jesus is for the Gentile. When will they offer God to the Jews?" And my thinking was, "Jesus the Son of God? Preposterous. Utterly illogical."

We discussed our dilemma endlessly.

Finally I suggested a possible solution. "Let's go discuss our situation with Pastor Spillman." By this time we had gotten acquainted with the Spillmans, Jim and Nancy, and felt quite comfortable with them. They had been especially kind to us, and, along with other couples our own age, we had enjoyed times of fellowship in their home.

Joan agreed with my suggestion. So we made the appointment for a week hence and arranged for a baby-sitter. However, on the evening of our appointment, the baby-sitter cancelled. It was too late to find someone else. What should we do? Should both of us stay home? Or should one go and leave the other with the kids?

Though I very much wanted to get some answers for my list of pastor stumpers, I told Joan to go. Then we'd make another appointment for both of us to go together. The date and time are indelibly engraved in my mind. It was August 16, 1970, one day after our sixth wedding anniversary. The time was 4:00 P.M. The place was Pastor Spillman's office at the church.

Joan was gone for a long time.

Mealtime came, and she hadn't returned. I prepared something for the kids and myself to eat, hoping Joan would be back in time to share it with us. But she didn't come. We finished the meal and did the dishes. Still Joan hadn't returned.

"When's Mommie coming home?" the kids asked.

"I don't know," I answered honestly. "She's at the church. She should be home soon."

Bedtime drew near. So I played with the kids for a while, gave them their baths, and put them in bed. Joan still hadn't returned. By now I was nervous and anxious. I went to the window and peered out, as though that would hasten her return. I picked up a book and tried to read, but couldn't concentrate.

I turned on the TV and played "channel roulette" for a while, but scarcely heard or saw anything. So I snapped it off and paced back and forth for a while. Where was she? What was happening? Why wasn't she home? I tried to imagine what was happening in Pastor Spillman's office. What could he be telling her that would take so long? Maybe I should have kept this first appointment instead of her.

Finally I heard the car drive up and the door slam. I grabbed the newspaper and sat down with it, trying to appear nonchalant.

Joan opened the door and entered. But she didn't

just *walk* in. She seemed to float. Judging from the big grin on her face, I knew she must have had a productive time with Pastor Spillman. She had been crying too, but that was nothing new for Joan when she went to church.

She closed the door and just stood there, looking at me, but not speaking. She seemed to radiate a heavenly something words could not describe.

Immediately I knew that something had happened. There was that same aura about her that surrounded Jack and LuAnn. She wore that same smile, that same other-worldly expression that was worn by those other Christians. By those *other* Christians? Could *it* have happened to my wife too?

In that moment I was suddenly, unaccountably lonely and empty. Like I'd lost my best friend. It was apparent that something had happened to her that I was not a part of. And in that long, wonderful, terrible moment I wondered if I ever could be a part of it, whatever it was. I could tell that Joan, my Jewish wife, knew something that I didn't know. Or possessed something that I didn't possess or even understand.

I don't know how long she stood there beaming at me. She seemed to be perfectly at ease and unutterably happy. She moved, but not toward me. She moved—or floated—into our bedroom. I couldn't stand it any longer. I dropped the newspaper on the floor and followed her.

She turned and faced me.

There was a new softness and radiant beauty about her.

Finally she spoke. "Hi, honey. I've got something to tell you. . . ."

I wanted to touch her, to hold her in my arms. But I

didn't. I don't know why. I just stood apart and looked at her.

"Oh, Steve . . ." she began. And I noticed that even the sound of her voice was different. "Steve, I've got so much to tell you." The words rushed out, tumbling over each other in their eagerness to be heard. "And I . . . I just don't know where to begin."

I was beseiged by a plethora of emotions. When I spoke, my voice didn't sound like my own. I sat down on the bed, cleared my throat, and began again. "Well . . . why don't you just start from the beginning."

Joan smiled and sat beside me. Even her smile and manner were somehow different. More loving and caring, it seemed. And there was a new gentleness about her.

"Well," she began, "I had to wait a few minutes, so I talked with Martha, Pastor Spillman's secretary. When Pastor Spillman called me into his office, I was a little nervous, but he put me at ease. He asked about you and the kids . . ."

That surprised me. "He did? What did he want to know?"

"Oh, just how things were at home. I told him things were okay. That they were fine."

I felt a surge of irritation. "Yeah, home's okay. It's the things in church that aren't so fine."

"I didn't tell him that," Joan said. "But he said he'd noticed that I cried in church, and he wondered why."

"What did you tell him?"

She shrugged. "I told him I didn't know exactly why, but that I just felt like crying sometimes. It wasn't that I was sad, but just sort of . . . well, overwhelmed by the message."

She paused and smiled up at me. I *liked* this new,

tender spirit in Joan. "I told him that I was Jewish and that I'd been raised in a Jewish home. I told him that as Jews our whole world, social and religious, revolved around the synagogue."

Pastor Spillman knew that Joan was Jewish, but he hadn't known to what extent. And he had chuckled when Joan told him of a conversation between her and her mother. "Mother asked me where we were attending services. When I told her Calvary Temple, she thought we were going to a synagogue."

Joan told Spillman of her frustration with the constant invitations to come to receive Jesus. "I told him that Jesus is for the Gentiles. All of my life I've wanted to know God, and to have everything he wanted for me. But I was never invited to know God . . . only Jesus. And I told him I didn't want to have anything to do with Jesus."

"How did Spillman respond to that?" I asked.

"He asked me why I didn't want to have anything to do with Jesus. I told him that I'd always been taught that Jesus was a good man and a good teacher. But since he claimed to be God, he was surely an impostor. I told him that the rabbis always warned us to avoid Christians who tried to force us to believe in Jesus."

I smiled to myself. Joan was standing up for herself. I asked, "What was Pastor Spillman's reaction to that?"

"He just smiled. He said, 'I'm not going to force you to do anything.' Then he opened his Bible and showed me God's plan for the Jews, how God has chosen them. I told him I was familiar with those Scriptures."

All the while she was speaking, Joan watched my eyes and face carefully. I knew she was trying to relate her experience carefully so I would be able to understand exactly what had happened. And I was listening intently to her every word. I knew that Pastor Spillman was a great Bible scholar, and that I would be talking to him soon. So I wanted to be prepared for his approach.

"But then, Steve, he showed me something I hadn't known before. He pointed out a lot of Old Testament Scriptures that promised the Jews a Messiah. Then he read the New Testament fulfillments of those promises. I was amazed!"

"How many did he show you?" I asked. "Three or four?"

"Oh, no. Many of them. More like twenty or so. And I learned that the Old Testament and the New Testament are one Book. I hadn't known that before. . . ."

She looked at me for confirmation, but I didn't answer.

"But I still didn't believe that Jesus was the Son of God," she went on, "because I remembered your argument that the New Testament was written by religious fanatics to support their Christian faith. So I wasn't totally convinced by Spillman."

"Good girl," I said. "I'm proud of you. You kept your head straight and didn't let him snow you. What happened then?"

Joan took a deep breath. "He said, 'Let's pray for you to receive Jesus as your Lord and Savior.' I started to cry a little, which disturbed him. I didn't want Jesus, but Pastor Spillman had been so sincere that I didn't see how I could refuse. . . ."

Joan looked up at me, and her eyes were glistening with unshed tears. She gripped my hand. "So we both knelt at a little prayer bench that he's got in his office. And . . . and that's when it happened."

135

I tried to hold my voice steady. "That's when *what* happened, Joanie?" I asked, searching my mind for what she meant.

"That's when Jesus came into my life! I looked at my watch, and it was exactly 5:30 P.M. And, oh, Steve, it was . . . it is . . . it's so wonderful. I feel like I'm just overflowing with God's love."

"Hey, wait a minute. Did I miss something?" I interrupted.

"What do you mean, honey?"

I was feeling angry at her illogical behavior. "I thought you were having trouble believing that Jesus Savior stuff. Yet you still prayed. And now you say he came into your life. What do you mean?"

Joan touched my arm in concern. "Please, let me explain. I wasn't paying any attention to Pastor Spillman as he prayed. I just closed my eyes and talked to God. I said, 'Lord, I want to know you. I want to have that joy and peace that I see in these people around me.' I told him, 'I don't believe that Jesus is the Messiah. And I could never believe in the virgin birth. But, God . . . I want to know you.' That's how I prayed, Steve."

I was still angry, and hurt, and lonely. But I didn't answer her at that point. I just nodded.

"And as I prayed," she went on, "I felt like . . . I'm not sure I can say it right. But I felt like I was being flooded with God's love. It felt like his joy and his peace just came over me and wrapped me in it. It was like . . . well, like the warmth from a fireplace . . . and that was when I knew . . ."

"Knew what?" I choked the words out. "What did you know?"

"Right at that moment I knew who Jesus Christ was, and is. I knew he was the Messiah, the Son of the Living God. I knew that he was truly born of a virgin. I knew that he lived and died for me . . . and that he was raised from the dead for me. And I knew that at that very moment he had come to live *in me*, so that I can have—and do have—eternal life."

It was a long speech for her. She paused and looked into my eyes for a moment, then went on. "And I felt so . . . so clean. So very clean . . ." She started to cry a little. "Oh, Steve, I know it sounds strange and irrational, but that's what happened. Please don't be angry with me. Please."

I tried to question her more, and she answered me kindly and sweetly. But her answers always came out the same way. And none of it made any sense to me. Finally I saw that I was getting nowhere, so we went to bed.

Lying rigidly in the dark I went over Joan's whole story bit by bit. After a while I conceded that she'd just had an emotional experience, and that it would soon pass. *This will all blow over and she'll come to her senses,* I told myself. Nevertheless, I was shaken and very upset.

I slept poorly.

14

IN THE VALLEY OF DECISION

For days my frustration and anger continued unabated. How could my wife, my *Jewish* wife at that, have accepted this Christianity thing? Especially since she was unable to explain the rationale behind her decision? Whenever I attempted to press or question her, she answered me the same way.

"I just *know* that I know," she would say. "And I'm more certain of Jesus than ever."

"Did Jim Spillman talk you into this thing?" I asked.

She shook her head. "No, he didn't try to talk me into anything. It was the revelation of the Holy Spirit."

"But how do you know?" I insisted.

"I just know."

She was so firm, so sweetly firm, in her conviction that I could not shake her. And finally I began to realize that there just *might be* some reality to the so-called "spiritual side" of man that we'd been hearing at Calvary Temple.

Frustrated and angry though I was, I could not help but notice the difference in Joan. She was a transformed person. And when I would allow myself to do so, I realized I was seeing in her the same qualities we had so admired in many of the Christians we had met at church. She evidenced a gentle sweetness, a constant joy, a love for all those around her, especially for me. All this, plus a confident boldness in her new Christian life.

All of these were qualities I desired for myself. But I wanted them on my own terms. By now I had my long list of pastor stumpers written down and ready for a confrontation. But I was beginning to wonder if I would ever get those questions answered. This possibility made me fearful. For if my questions were not to receive satisfactory answers, except by somehow gaining the knowledge I sought "in my spirit," as Joan talked about, I feared that I would have lost my mind and my credibility as an engineer. Then my career would be at an end.

I began to ask some of my fellow workers about their views of God. To my surprise, there was a wide variance of thinking. My supervisor was a Christian who, thanks to Jack, knew what I was going through. Though I liked him immensely, he frequently told me, "Steve, if you don't accept Jesus as your Savior, you're doomed to go to hell when you die."

The engineer who occupied the desk behind me was an older man whom I respected. Jack told me that this man was also a Christian; in fact, he was the organist in his church. I asked this man if he believed the Genesis account.

He shook his head. "I believe man evolved just as the evolutionists tell it, except that at some point God breathed life into man's nostrils. And at that time man received his spiritual nature."

I thought for a moment. "But if you believe that, how can you believe that the Bible is true from cover to cover?"

"We don't believe the Bible is literally true, but that it's just a collection of stories and historic lessons."

The discovery that not all Christians accepted the total veracity of the Bible opened a Pandora's box for me. Nevertheless, I was evidently making some progress. I now accepted the good, moral teachings of the Scriptures. I could even believe that most of the recorded history was true and accurate. But I still could not accept as truth the "fables, myths, and miracles." I considered them to have come from the unscientific minds and pens of authors who wanted to support their own man-made ideas of a Supreme Being.

Jack and I spent many a late evening in the Martin Marietta parking lot discussing this "accept-the-parts-of-the-Bible-you-want-to" concept. And in that series of discussions, I zeroed in on what I consider to be Christianity's most attractive concept: its absolute standard of rightness. In an age where all standards seem to have deteriorated to the "situational ethics" level, this truth was, to me, equivalent to the discovery of a gold mine. I admitted to Jack and to myself that such a standard—which had remained unchanged for thousands of years—if accepted and followed, would still guide a person into an excellent, unselfish life-style.

Jack agreed with me. "However," he pointed out, "if that standard is to be the standard, then it must remain the standard. *In one piece.* If you begin to toss out this or that, even a very small portion of Scripture, just because it doesn't agree with your way of thinking, then you've destroyed the absoluteness of the Bible as a reference standard."

This was a huge bite to swallow, but I could certainly see the truth involved in Jack's rationale.

Meanwhile, life at home was proceeding apace, though somewhat different than previously. For one thing, Joan began talking about things that "God had arranged" for us. And she would excitedly tell me about these miraculous "answers to prayer." But in each case I insisted that these "arrangements" and "answers" were merely coincidences.

There were times, though, when I was forced to admit that some of these "coincidences" were very unlikely.

Like the time when Pastor Spillman announced that he was going to take a few weeks off to move to a new house. With a family of five children, this would certainly be a major task. But when we asked him where he was going to move, he said, "I don't know the address. The Lord hasn't given us a new home yet."

I thought this was a most outlandish, unbusinesslike manner with which to approach such a serious matter. But both Jim and Nancy assured us that the Lord had often performed a miracle for them when they moved, each time supplying them with a house "just the right size."

But during the time the Spillmans were away from Calvary Temple in the process of moving, Joan decided she just must talk to Pastor Jim. The fact is, she wanted to discuss with him how she was to lead her stubborn, technically-minded husband to accept Jesus. She had sensed a certain "softening" of my heart, and she wanted to tell Pastor Jim about it. There was only one problem: nobody knew where Pastor Jim was.

So Joan began praying that the Lord would lead her to him.

He did so (she claimed) in a most unusual, round-about way. Joan had just discovered that she was pregnant with our third child, and our small rented home would no longer be adequate for our growing family. So while I was away on one of my frequent business trips, Joan decided to look for another house.

She was convinced that the first house she saw was much too expensive for us, and she thought to herself, "Why should I even look at it?" But somehow she just "felt" that she should go see it; so she made an appointment with the realtor. As it turned out, when she toured the property, the house was too large and too expensive for our budget.

However—and this is how God "coincidentally" answered Joan's prayer—when she stepped out of the house, she noticed a familiar figure next door unloading groceries from his car: Pastor Spillman. We argued about such coincidental events for weeks, neither of us successfully convincing the other of his point of view.

Another different "business as usual" procedure at our home from that evening of her "landmark" decision was that Joan had developed an insatiable hunger for the Bible. Prior to her confrontation with Jesus, we had both read the Bible sporadically, but without much comprehension. Now I would often see her with an open Bible, a notebook, and a pen. And she was actually *marking* in the Bible (something I would never do), and making notes in her notebook as she read.

One evening I saw her cutting some preprinted cards from sheets of card stock, pausing to read each one as she did.

"What are those?" I asked.

"They're Scripture memory cards," she told me.

"Scripture memory cards!" I burst out. "What are they for?"

"The Bible tells us, 'Thy Word have I hid in my heart that I might not sin . . . ,'" she said. "So I'm using these little cards to help me memorize God's Word. Look, each one has a different verse printed on one side, with the reference on the other."

I picked up one of the cards and read aloud, "Trust in the Lord with all thine heart: and lean not unto thine own understanding . . ." There was more, but what I'd read made me angry. I threw the card down.

"What's the matter?" Joan asked, startled at my action.

"Just look at that, Joan," I burst out. "Look at it and *listen* to what it says."

"What do you mean?"

"That Scripture is telling us not to think for ourselves. That's just like the Bible. It tells us not to use our minds. Just 'have faith.' Just 'trust me,'" I mimicked God.

Joan paled. "But, Steve, that doesn't mean . . ."

"I can read what it means, Joan!" I interrupted angrily. "It says, don't trust your own mind. Joanie, that's all I've got: my mind. I've spent all my life training my mind to think rationally, and now the Bible tells me not to use it. Am I supposed to park my brain outside the door when I go to church? I've had it with this God stuff!" And I stormed out of the room, slamming the door behind me, my usual routine when I was upset.

Being the loving, patient wife that she is, Joan allowed me to cool off for a while, then found me. I was trying to calm my troubled spirit by strumming on my guitar. She came and sat on the arm of the chair and hugged me. Neither of us spoke for a few minutes, but I sensed her hurting, just as she sensed mine.

Our hurts were different. She hurt because she longed for me to see in Christ what she saw. I knew that she hurt for me, and that she was concerned for me and our relationship during this awkward time.

I hurt because I was confused and frustrated and angry. But even in the midst of my confusion and hurt, I was now convinced that Joan's experience was not temporary. It was not about to go away. She had made a firm decision, one that she would abide by.

I idly strummed a few chords while Joan caressed my arm. When she spoke it was without rancor. Her voice was warm with love and caring.

"Honey," she began, "why don't you go see Pastor Spillman? There's no need for you to keep being angry. Go to him and get some straight answers. You can take your pastor stumpers with you. He may not have all the answers, but I think he can help you find them. . . ."

I strummed a few more chords before I answered.

Joan was so different now. I had watched her carefully during these past weeks since she'd become a converted Jew, or Christian Jew, or completed Jew, or whatever. All of these were terms I'd heard from various churchgoers. She was so serene. And she spoke with such assurance, such wisdom, such love.

All along I had known what the answer to my dilemma must be. I knew it now. But I hated to think that I'd have to share an experience such as Joan's to find the peace I longed for and the other attributes she possessed.

I ran my fingers across the strings and put the guitar down. "You're right, Joan. I should go see Pastor Spillman." I looked up at her. "Will you make the appointment for me?"

She smiled. "Of course."

15

PASTOR STUMPERS

The appointment was set for the following Wednesday evening just prior to the midweek service. I spent a lot of time preparing for this meeting. My list of pastor stumpers was complete. I patted my coat pocket to be sure it was there. Promptly on time Joan and I entered Pastor Spillman's office.

I ran my eyes a little nervously over the office furniture, lighting on the piece Joan had referred to as the "prayer bench." I made a mental note that it was there, on that spot, where the change had taken place in Joan.

Pastor Spillman, appearing easy and relaxed, seated us in front of his huge wooden desk and positioned himself in his desk chair. I was as tense as a spring, but primed and ready for the fray. I was pleased that Joan had come with me. I still retained a vestige of hope that she would return to her senses once she witnessed a logical dialogue concerning this "God business."

Pastor Spillman spoke first. "Steve, what do you think of your new wife?"

"I think she's just great. But the old wife wasn't too bad either." I smiled at Joan and gave her hand a squeeze.

"You must have noticed quite a difference in her."

"Yes, she has changed. For one thing, she reads the Bible a lot." I refrained from delineating Joan's many new qualities.

He grinned. "Well, Joan told me that you've got a lot of questions you'd like answered. . . ."

Here was my long-awaited opportunity. "Right," I said, reaching for my list.

"Before we get to your questions, Steve, may I ask *you* one question?"

That seemed fair enough, and harmless enough. I thought he wanted to ask me another question about my work, because he had always been interested in "spacebiz," as he called it. I pulled my hand back from my pocket.

Pastor Spillman leaned toward me. Looking me directly in the eye, he asked, "Steve, are you ready to accept Jesus Christ as your Lord and Savior?"

It was a direct hit, and it exploded in my mind. I reeled with the punch for what seemed an eternity. As I tried to marshal my forces, the thought came, *Why would he ask such a thing? He knows about my questions. And he knows I won't accept Jesus until I get satisfactory answers. This . . . this isn't fair. Not fair at all.*

Then, like one of the computers I worked with, my mental machinery recovered, and the answer to Pastor Spillman's question flashed like a neon light. *No . . . no . . . no!* it flashed. But I could not force the words out of my mouth. It was as though I was in a tailspin. My speaking mechanism was out of control.

I looked at Joan, who knew the answer I would normally give. In that brief moment I saw her smile tighten to a serious look, then to a slight frown. Still no word came from my mouth. Joan was watching me. Pastor Spillman fixed me with his eyes. His unanswered question hung in the air.

For some reason I could not fathom, my mind replayed that Scripture verse of Joan's that I had ridiculed and thrown down. "Trust in the Lord with all your heart, and lean not unto your own understanding. . . ." The words echoed in my head.

In a millisecond of time the message of that verse triggered my mind to reconsider my response to the question, and a thought flashed on my screen. *Suppose that is the right answer, the key? Trust—the "blind faith" that I found so abhorrent.* That would seem to fit the evidence. Joan had had to "trust" in God before she "knew." Why hadn't I seen that before?

My mouth fluttered to answer in accord with the thought.

Then it clamped shut again. *Don't be too hasty, Steve. How can you justify any answer but no?*

The verse flashed on my screen again: "Don't lean to your own understanding. . . ."

That's it, I thought. *I'll conduct a scientific experiment. I'll try the "faith" route like Joan did. Then I'll see if there is any validity in what she's been telling me.*

That scene remains frozen in my memory. I was in that little room, but it seemed to have expanded. Joan was there, looking at me. Pastor Spillman was there, leaning toward me, awaiting my answer. I opened my mouth and a word came out. As though from a great distance I heard myself utter my answer.

"Yes."

Instantly I felt stupid and out of control. *How could I have compromised my mind, my most trusted asset?* I asked myself. *Why did I say that?* I couldn't answer. Suddenly I felt panic. Where would I go from here? What would this mean? What would I do? What would happen? I felt like shouting, "No! No, I'm not ready for this. Wait! Stop!"

But it was already too late to turn back. I had answered yes to a no question.

I was aware that Joan's mouth had opened wide. Her face was wreathed in a lovely smile; tears were forming in her eyes. But Pastor Spillman's expression hadn't changed. He acted as though I had given the expected answer and was playing the script exactly as written.

Calm and unruffled, he opened his Bible.

"Steve," he said, "in order to accept Jesus, you must pray the 'Sinner's Prayer.' " Then he began to read, " 'For all have sinned and come short of the glory of God.' "

Suddenly I came up with a reason to interrupt this charade. "Wait a minute, Pastor," I said, "I'm not a sinner."

Pastor Spillman paused and looked up expectantly.

"I've never killed anybody. I've never fooled around with anybody else's wife. I've never stolen anything. . . ." I was desperately trying to recall the Ten Commandments. I honestly didn't think I'd been bad enough to be considered a "sinner." Although our marriage had been rocky at times, basically it was very sound.

Pastor Spillman waited until I ran down, then asked simply, "Steve, has an evil thought ever crossed your mind?"

His response puzzled me. "What's that got to do with being a sinner?" I asked.

He opened his Bible to another place and read words I'd never heard. "Steve, Jesus says that even to think about sinning is equivalent to the very act itself."

I was stunned. I had no way to respond to Pastor Spillman's statement. If what he had just read me was true, and I had no doubt but that it was, then I was guilty. I was a sinner, and as such I had need of help. I needed someone to redeem me. I needed a Savior.

Pastor Spillman patiently explained what I needed to do. "Steve, when we pray, admit to God that you're a sinner. Ask him for his forgiveness. Ask Jesus Christ to come in and take over your life. Then accept him into your heart."

I heard Pastor Spillman's words, but they seemed to come from a great distance. A heaviness had settled over me that I couldn't understand. I was suddenly weary, almost too weary to move. I had never felt like this before. I looked up at Pastor Spillman helplessly.

I was aware that he'd stopped talking.

He arose and so did Joan. Hardly aware of the effort of doing so, I arose too. Pastor Spillman motioned for Joan and me to join him at the prayer bench. Vaguely I realized this must be the very place where Joan had knelt a few weeks ago.

"Let's pray here," Pastor Spillman said, indicating that I kneel in the middle.

Joan knelt on one side of me and Pastor Spillman on the other. The thought came to me, *If God actually exists, I will give him a chance.* The moment I knelt and opened my mouth, something within me seemed to burst, and I cried to God aloud for the first time in my life. I was twenty-seven years old, but I heard words spilling from my lips with the same kind of hesitation I'd expect from a third-grader.

Without coaching, I earnestly prayed, "God, if you are real, please let me know it. . . . Whatever you've given to Joan, that's what I want. . . . Lord, I know I am a sinner, and I ask you to please forgive my sins. . . ."

The words seemed to come from some deep cavern inside me. "Jesus . . . Jesus [it seemed strange for me, Steve Carman, to use that name in prayer] . . . I give my life to you. I now open my heart and ask you to come in and take over my life . . . just as I am."

Even as I prayed those words, they seemed simplistic and juvenile to my scientific mind and ear. But somehow that didn't seem to matter. I paused and thought about what I'd said. I felt little different than when I'd knelt down.

I took a deep breath and began again. "God, if you are real and if you've heard my prayer, please help me to trust you. Please help me to have faith in you. Please help me to understand the answers to my many questions."

There was still no "evidence" that my words had gone anywhere. Then I said the words that seemed to be wrung from the very essence of my being. "I want to believe in you, but you know that my mind gets in the way."

I'm not sure what I was expecting, perhaps a bolt of lightning and a crash of thunder. Those would have been nice signs. But they didn't come.

Instead came something even more meaningful: I sensed a voice—not with my ears, but nonetheless very real. And that voice conveyed to me words of immense worth and meaning. "Steve, you *can* believe in me. *I am real.*"

It was a moment of revelation.

I was overwhelmed with a feeling of love. I was aware of goosebumps all over my body, and I began to weep for joy. I prayed again that he would come and take over every area, every detail of my life. And in that moment I understood what Joan had tried so hard to explain to me. I knew something real and vital had happened.

But I also realized that I would be no more able to rationally explain it than Joan had been.

That no longer seemed to matter.

As I basked in the warmth of what I now realized was God's love, I was as certain of the reality of God as I was of the reality of the bench I was kneeling on. I heard the sweet voice of my wife praying for me. I heard Pastor Jim Spillman praying. I looked at my watch. It was 6:42 p.m., September 2, 1970. That was when my dead spirit was awakened, reborn, made alive.

It was a new Steve Carman who stood to his feet. I was aware that much had transpired during the past few minutes, so much that it would take weeks or longer to put it all into perspective. I was still a space scientist, but I was now a new and somehow different space scientist. I would have to figure all of that out, too. But I was new and clean and peaceful. And full of love.

I was aware that I was sobbing unashamedly. I was euphoric. Joan hugged me, and I saw the tears glistening on her cheeks. It was a tremendous moment that seemed to stand still for a long, long, meaningful eternity.

Pastor Jim Spillman broke the spell. With his huge, lovely smile and typical chuckle, he said, "And now, Steve . . . you said something about some questions?"

I had totally forgotten my pastor stumpers. I felt my breast-coat pocket. They were still there. I shook my head. "Not now, Pastor," I said. "We'll get to them another time."

EPILOGUE

"A totally new dimension of life was unveiled to us when Joan and I opened ourselves up to Jesus," Steve said. "And as a result of that new beginning, our good marriage became great as we learned the true meaning of love. Our close family drew even closer as we made Jesus the center of our lives. Our lives have been enriched beyond measure, for which we are very grateful."

Instead of losing his credibility as an aerospace engineer (which he had feared) when he opened himself up to God's will and received Jesus as his Savior, Steve Carman has found himself continually promoted to new projects on the cutting edge of space science. As he learned to apply Christ's teachings to his attitude toward work, Steve became known as an unflappable, excellent engineering manager with a gentle sense of humor. One of his fellow workers once said, "Steve always seems to draw his strength and wisdom from a higher source."

The last chapter closed with Steve Carman and his

Messianic Jewish wife living in Denver, where the two
of them had just turned over their lives to God. Since
that time nothing has remained static. The week after
Steve accepted Christ, Pastor Jim Spillman had Steve
share his testimony in the Wednesday evening service.
Steve's story burst like a bombshell in Calvary Temple,
resulting in weeks of speaking engagements before a
wide variety of churches and other religious groups.

"It seemed that everybody wanted to hear what had
happened to the atheistic space scientist and his Jewish
wife who came to believe in God," Steve said. "Besides
that, despite our lack of Bible knowledge, Joan and I
often were invited to teach Bible studies to various
groups. We fortunately had such a thirst for the Word
that we started a Bible study for beginners in our
home, where we could immerse ourselves in the Scriptures. We rapidly grew to understand the basics, and
then ventured into deeper areas."

Steve especially studied the Scriptures relating to the
questions he had written down to ask Pastor Spillman.
Those questions didn't go away or lose his interest. On
the contrary, they became the focus of many years of
digging, reading, and prayer. Finally, after about seven
years of study, Steve satisfied his technical mind that
the biblical account does not conflict with science, but
instead he found that science could bring a greater understanding to God's Word than ever before.

Today, both Steve and Joan are in demand as speakers for churches, retreats, and seminars. Steve teaches
on various aspects of science and the Bible, during
which he answers those same "pastor stumper" questions that bothered him for so long: and he frequently
appears on Christian television in that regard.

Joan and Steve also studied the history of Judaism and searched for an understanding of the Jewish people and their attitude toward Christ, who was, after all, a Jew. Out of their study grew another aspect of their ministry, which they share together. Each year Steve and Joan conduct numerous Christian Passover dinners (seders) and demonstrations which introduce the participants to an understanding of the rich heritage Christians have in Judaism, particularly in the Jewish holiday traditions.

Professionally, Steve Carman has risen steadily to ever-increasing positions of responsibility on various projects in the nation's space program. He moved his family to Florida for a year while he participated in the final checkout and launch of the Viking spacecraft to Mars. Then they went to California—where they now live—when Steve was selected to participate in supervising the Viking Mars mission as part of the team of scientists and engineers at the Jet Propulsion Laboratory. For the past several years he has held the title of senior project engineer in the Advanced Products Laboratory of TRW's Space and Technology Group in Redondo Beach, California.

As coauthor, during the rather lengthy process of preparing this manuscript for publication, it has been my privilege to become intimately acquainted with the Carmans, whom I now consider to be good friends. And each time we have met, whether in a television studio, a restaurant, or our respective homes or offices, I have been impressed with Steve's vast knowledge of engineering and space science.

But even more than that, I am deeply impressed with

Steve's quiet confidence in the absolute veracity of God's Word. In a day when so many are bowing to altars created by atheistic scientists, it is refreshing to meet a man of Steve's stature who believes, and confidently speaks to all, that our God, the Creator of this vast universe, is alive and well!